ACTIVE
NYMPHING

ACTIVE NYMPHING

AGGRESSIVE STRATEGIES
for Casting, Rigging, and Moving Nymphs

Rich Osthoff

STACKPOLE
BOOKS

Dedicated to Aaron Cox on behalf of his wife, Vivian.

Published by
STACKPOLE BOOKS
5067 Ritter Road
Mechanicsburg, PA 17055
www.stackpolebooks.com

Cover photograph by Rich Osthoff
Cover design by Caroline Stover
Photographs by Rich Osthoff, except where otherwise noted
Illustrations by Dave Hall

Library of Congress Cataloging-in-Publication Data

Osthoff, Rich.
    Active nymphing : aggressive strategies for casting, rigging, and moving nymphs / Rich Osthoff. — 1st ed.
       p. cm.
    ISBN-13: 978-0-8117-3255-0
    ISBN-10: 0-8117-3255-X
    1. Nymph fishing.   I. Title.
SH456.15O88 2005
799.12'2—dc22

                                                         2005018498

CONTENTS

ACKNOWLEDGMENTS

I owe a special thanks to fellow fly-fishing writer Dave Hughes. Dave has gone out of his way to be supportive of my writing even before I had the privilege of meeting him.

During his reign as editor at *American Angler* and *Fly Tyer* magazines, Art Sheck published almost everything I sent him, including my first unsolicited piece. My appreciation to Art for helping me break in.

My gratitude to Judith Schnell, editorial director at Stackpole Books, for her support and guidance.

PREFACE

Nymphing. There are two ways to approach it: as a rote technique for dredging up a few trout between hatches, or as your ticket to becoming a truly versatile and productive fly fisher. No other form of fly fishing has broader application throughout the season on so many water types for both active and inactive trout, including those elusive top-end fish that are measured in pounds rather than inches and so often specialize in feeding subsurface.

Nymphing as most anglers learn and practice it, dead drifting a short line, is really only a single facet of nymphing. Indeed, over the course of a season, I catch many more trout by actively moving the nymph than I do by dead drifting. Moving a nymph, especially a substantial attractor tied with lively materials, often triggers loads of reflexive or aggressive strikes, even from trout that are not particularly interested in feeding. And we all encounter trout in that mode much of the time.

The most versatile nymph fishers are skilled dead drifters, but they also routinely employ wet-fly and streamer tactics to activate the nymph and agitate nonfeeding trout into striking. During many of my hottest sessions, I turn upstream dead-drift nymphing on its ear by working downstream and keeping the imitation moving almost constantly as I swim it across the snouts of inactive trout that are sulking near the bottom in refuge areas. And you haven't experienced electrifying nymphing and jolting strikes until you've worked downstream or across current to highly aggressive trout in off-color water, a frequent occurrence on spring creeks in many regions as streams drop and clear in the wake of storms. Fly fishers who can skillfully play the downstream angles can simultaneously activate a nymph as they hang or delay its progression through prime pockets, and that's a deadly one-two combination that will have you tearing up dirty water when most anglers, including conventional dead-drift nymphers, are whining about "unfishable" conditions. Favorable water temperatures and off-color water—not like chocolate milk, but with restricted visibility— will usually set the stage for dynamic nymphing.

Then there is the demanding game of long-line nymphing for active trout in gin-clear spring creeks, a form of nymphing that brings a host of precision skills to bear, including casting weighted nymphs at significant ranges with high line speeds and dry-fly accuracy. Invigorating water temperatures often move spring-creek trout from deeper refuge water into relatively shallow feeding stations, even in the absence of a hatch. To avoid spooking small-stream fish in clear water, you often must work from far enough away that nymphing becomes a horizontal game rather than the vertical one to which most anglers are accustomed. And once you've refined your horizontal nymphing skills on small streams, you'll recognize plenty of opportunities to put them into play on sizable rivers, where the fishing can be remarkably similar to small streams when active trout are moving from deep to shallow water. In fact, when big, brawling rivers like Montana's Madison really turn on, you can often mop up by long-line nymphing the skinny water where most guys are wading.

There is also the fascinating world of nymphing for trout in stillwater, where the fish actively cruise for their food rather than patrol fixed stations as they do in current. If, like many fly fishers, you're not all that interested in fishing lakes, you might want to reconsider. Trout routinely grow larger in lakes than they do in rivers, and many phenomenal trout lakes are neglected even though they sit right next door to famed and overcrowded rivers. Plenty of big trout on public water without another angler in sight should not be ignored. Many big-time trout rivers, such as the Green River below Flaming Gorge in Utah, have big back eddies where trout routinely cruise for food, just as they do in lakes. Anglers armed with lake-nymphing savvy can successfully target eddy cruisers even when main flows are fishing poorly. As when encountering any new water type, fishing lakes entails learning new tactics, and these will transfer to other waters. Fishing extensively on lakes drilled home to me the value of activating nymphs to grab the attention of trout and generate strikes, even from nonfeeding fish—knowledge that I now routinely employ on moving water.

Nymphing, like dry-fly fishing, has both attractor and imitative forms. Imitative, match-the-natural nymphing has broad application for bracketing hatches and fishing subsurface during hatches, where the most efficient and largest trout often gorge on emerging nymphs and pupae while ignoring food on the surface. Matching the hatch with emerging nymphs fished on or near the surface is essentially dry-fly nymphing, with all of the satisfaction of visual takes—and a lot more takes than you would get by fishing dry flies during some hatches.

Even standard dead-drift nymphing, which many fly fishers dismiss as boring, runs the gamut from bouncing heavily weighted nymphs on the bottom in considerable current to suspending tiny micronymphs beneath buoyant indicators and creeping them through slow-water refuge areas at precisely controlled depths. Micronymphing is often the key to steady action between hatches on tremendously fertile tailwater rivers, such as the San Juan, but it also transfers exceptionally well to small spring creeks where inactive trout typically stack up in confined refuge slots.

There's really no limit to how creative you can become with your presentations and strategies. And as you begin to understand that nymphing is not merely a single rote technique for dredging up a few fish between hatches, but an entire set of intricate skills to employ in an array of situations, your versatility and productivity as an angler will soar. You won't just catch a few more trout—you'll catch a lot more trout on a lot more days, including a lot more top-end fish. And while you are expanding your skills, you will come to enjoy nymphing on entirely new levels—the casting, the presentation, the strategy, the results.

Before you know it, you'll be fishing dry flies only when conditions warrant.

CHAPTER 1

Rigging

In order to probe the depths with your nymph and not just skim the surface, you need to employ weight to sink it. There are three primary ways to do this: by adding weight to the nymph at the tying vise, by adding weight to the tippet on the water, or by using a sinking fly line, to which weight or density has been added by the manufacturer. Of the three methods, adding weight to the tippet is generally the most versatile and efficient way to sink a nymph in current, where most nymphing for trout is done. Why adding weight to the tippet is so often singled out as something less than true fly fishing eludes me, but I suspect it has at least as much to do with the inability of many fly fishers to cast weighted rigs with precision and ease (a critical nymphing skill) as it does with angling ethics. And ethically speaking, I don't see a drop of difference in whether it's the fly line, the fly, or the tippet that is weighted. It's all added weight intended to sink the fly. So why not choose the method that's best suited to the conditions at hand?

SINKING FLY LINES

Sinking fly lines have their place in nymphing. In my view, that place is primarily on stillwater and to a lesser extent on sizable rivers with long, spacious runs. Sinking lines have several significant drawbacks for nymphing in current. Given their considerable diameter, they are prone to being transported horizontally by the current as they sink. That makes it difficult to drop a nymph straight down with a sinking line in heavy current, in turbulent pocket water, off deep cutbanks, or where riffles shelve abruptly into depths—exactly the kinds of situations that abound on most moving trout water and call for a fast vertical sink.

More often than not, you want to sink a nymph quickly in current to put it in the productive bottom zone throughout the drift. If the prime fish-holding slot in a run is only 6 feet long, but it takes 5 feet of downstream drift to sink the nymph near bottom, you're fishing over the top of most bottom-hugging trout. If the sweet spot in a run is 30 feet long, then using 5 feet of drift to sink the nymph near bottom still leaves you with 25 feet of productive drift, making sinking lines better suited to nymphing long runs than short ones.

But there are significant secondary drawbacks to nymphing with sinking lines in current, even on sizable water. For starters, the weight of a sinking line is fixed, so it can't be readily altered on a run-by-run basis for a faster or slower sink rate as you work your way through a variety of depths and current speeds.

Also, an unweighted nymph tied to a conventional leader drifts up to several feet above the tip of a sinking fly line. You can keep the nymph closer to the depth of the line tip by using a very short leader, but that rig is highly susceptible to drag and poorly suited to dead-drift nymphing. Since sinking lines don't accommodate strike indicators, dead-drift strike detection is difficult, even for experienced anglers.

The increased slap of sinking lines on the surface makes them prone to spooking trout on the slick water that alternates with the quick water on most streams. When you couple a sinking line with a short leader, you'll spook many smooth-water trout by inadvertently dropping the fly line directly atop them, particularly as you prospect with upstream casts.

Sinking lines and short leaders are really best suited for swinging and stripping nymphs, wet flies, and streamers on downstream or across-current presentations that put the fly in the point position so that it arrives at the fish ahead of the line and leader. However, when nymphing downstream or across-current, I find that I can usually manipulate the fly even more precisely and enticingly with a floating line and weighted tippet. This same combination is well suited for conventional upstream dead-drift nymphing and sinking a nymph vertically in plunge pools, off cutbanks, along drop-offs, or under snags, giving me great flexibility in my presentations as I work my way along a stream through a variety of water types. And that's a very big advantage. Flexibility in your presentations is critical to becoming a creative and versatile nymph fisher who can pick moving water apart on a run-by-run and station-by-station basis.

In this book, I discuss various nymphing techniques separately for the sake of clarity. But in reality, as you work your way along moving water, you need to employ a range of techniques to deal with the changing depths, changing current speeds, changing angles and ranges of presentation, and changing moods of the trout. Even if you nymph primarily on a single stream type, such as small freestone streams, versatility in your presentations is still critical to effectively cover all of the productive water types that occur there.

Never underestimate the value of throwing the trout a pattern and presentation that they're not accustomed to seeing. Unorthodox nymphing tactics are particularly productive on hard-fished kill waters, where the only trout that survive to maturity have something out of the ordinary going for them, such as exceptional wariness or a lie where it is especially tricky to hook or land them. On the premier special-regulation waters, a high percentage of the trout are big, but they are also extremely wary from being fished over by a steady stream of anglers, many of whom are fresh from the local fly shops and armed with the same hot flies and the same sage advice on where and how to fish them. On heavily fished water, I'm always looking to do something different from other anglers, including showing the fish a pattern and presentation that they're not largely inoculated against.

WEIGHTING NYMPHS
Tying your own flies puts you in control of every aspect of fly design, including whether and how you weight your nymphs. But even if you buy your nymphs, the same weighting considerations apply.

Micronymphs, a term I apply broadly to subsurface imitations in size 18 and smaller, are generally too small for tiers to add weighting wire to the hook shank without adding undesirable bulk to the finished fly. The same is true with many slender imitative mayfly nymphs and midge larvae in sizes 14 to 16. Micronymphs and minimally tied midsize nymphs pick up a bit of weight from the hook itself and from copper wire or other fine-diameter ribbings, but sinking them quickly in substantial current requires weighting the tippet or using a sinking line. But dead drifting the really small stuff with sinking lines is problematic, which pretty much leaves weighting the tippet as the most versatile and effective method.

Most size 14 and larger nymphs are robust enough to accommodate foundation wraps of weighting wire on the hook shank, but there are differing schools of thought regarding weighting nymphs at the vise. Not weighting them gives greater flexibility on the water. For example, an unweighted Hare's Ear can be fished in the surface film as an emerger during a mayfly hatch or tumbled along the bottom as a prospecting nymph with the aid of split shot on the tippet. You can always add weight to the tippet or use a sinking line to sink an unweighted nymph, but you can't remove foundation wraps from the hook shank of a weighted nymph to fish it in or near the surface.

Even nymphs that are intended to be tumbled along the bottom almost exclusively, such as big stonefly nymph imitations, are often best tied unweighted or lightly weighted, because the most efficient method is to have your weight contact the bottom periodically and your nymph riding slightly above. This presents the nymph right at the feeding level of bottom-hugging fish, and you'll hang up less frequently if you have round shot or putty bouncing on the bottom rather than a pointed hook. Natural nymphs are close to neutral in buoyancy, and an unweighted imitation that's free to float upward a bit closely mimics a natural that has lost its purchase and is drifting just off the bottom.

So should all nymphs be tied unweighted? No. But as a rule, tying nymphs unweighted gives you the flexibility to fish them at any depth and lets them drift more naturally and efficiently near the bottom. I tie all of my micronymphs and many midsize imitative nymphs, such as my Pheasant Tail Nymphs, unweighted so that I can fish them as emergers in or near the surface or drift them deeper with the aid of weight on the tippet.

Most of my bread-and-butter prospecting nymphs are buggy, robust ties that I'm not concerned about fishing right in the surface film as hatch-matching emergers, so I weight them lightly with about eight wraps of wire on the hook shank. That allows me to sink them a bit without adding split shot to the tippet, and for many flat-water and stillwater situations,

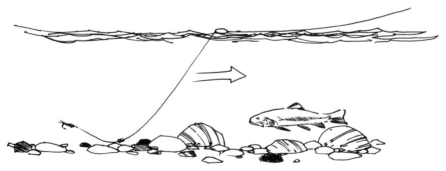

The most snag-free and productive method of bouncing on the bottom is with your weight contacting the bottom periodically and your unweighted or lightly weighted nymph riding slightly above. Positioning shot within about 8 inches of the nymph keeps the fly in the productive bottom zone and minimizes fouled rigs when casting at high line speeds.

stripping a lively nymph just subsurface is the hot ticket. When I need to get these lightly weighted prospecting nymphs down quickly in current, which is much of the time, I add shot to the tippet as needed. I find that in significant current, lightly weighted nymphs still buoy up quite effectively as the heavier shot or putty ticks bottom.

For fishing in current, I don't weight any of my nymphs heavily on the hook shank, although for lakes I weight a few specialty nymphs heavily. Even my big size 4 and 6 prospecting and stonefly nymphs I weight only lightly for flexible presentations in various current speeds and depths and for a natural-looking dead drift. I define lightly weighted as about eight wraps of lead wire equal in diameter to the hook shank. If you're using lighter nontoxic wire or lead wire that's significantly thinner than the hook wire, you'll need more wraps to achieve equivalent weight. On size 12 to 16 nymphs, I generally use .015-inch wire; on size 8 and 10 nymphs, .020-inch wire; and on size 6 and larger nymphs, .025-inch wire.

The design of a nymph plays into its sink rate. I tie most of my prospecting nymphs very robustly, with soft, webby hen hackle and spiky hare-blend bodies, and all of that spike and web increases surface area and hydraulic friction, slowing the sink rate of the nymph. These exceptionally rough and buggy prospecting nymphs require more weight just to punch through the surface tension and begin sinking. Even with a dozen wraps of foundation wire, they sink quite slowly without the aid of shot on the leader. Conversely, sparsely tied flies sink much faster with less weight on the hook shank or tippet.

These nymph-weighting recommendations are not set in stone. One of the big advantages of tying your own nymphs is that you control their weighting. So play around with the weighting wire to see what works best for you. To compare bottom-bouncing results between heavily weighted and unweighted or lightly weighted nymphs fished with the aid of weight on the tippet, tie several versions with different head colors so that you can identify them at a glance. Varying your thread and head colors is a handy way to code how all of your nymphs are weighted.

No discussion of weighting nymphs is complete without addressing beadheads. I've heard beadhead nymphs disparaged as nothing more than fly-rod jigs. Actually, I find that the copper beads used on most nymphs do not increase sink rate all that dramatically. In fact, I would describe a size 12 Hare's Ear Nymph tipped with a typical ⅛-inch copper bead and no additional weight as lightly weighted. Certainly the bead enhances the sink rate, but it does not by itself sink the nymph quickly in substantial current or impart bona fide jigging properties, unless it's an oversize or heavy tungsten bead on a minimally tied fly. I believe that the effectiveness of beadhead nymphs stems more from the flash of the bead than from its weight. In fact, more often than not, I fish beadhead nymphs with additional split shot on the tippet to sink them quickly to desired depths.

Lead eyes and conehead weights are typically heavy enough to sink nymphs and streamers nose-first and quite vertically, even in strong current. You can rig any nymph to plummet nose-first by sliding a heavy split shot tight to the hook eye, and I sometimes do that, but shot does not deliver the attractive color or flash of painted or plated weights. I usually carry a few robust prospecting nymphs and streamers tipped with heavy lead eyes or coneheads for achieving a very fast vertical sink in swift pockets, including the turbulent pools found at the bases of plunges and falls.

Lead eyes and coneheads make nymphs so nose-heavy that they can be stripped or pumped with an erratic hopping action. Hopping a nymph often triggers aggressive strikes, even from inactive trout. Lead eyes lashed on top of a hook shank generally cause a nymph to roll over and ride with the hook point up, making it more snag-resistant than other heavily weighted nymphs. For hopping a nymph directly across silt bottoms and kicking up fish-attracting plumes, lead eyes are ideal. Trout certainly aren't offended that this is basically a jigging action. Natural organisms such as crayfish and sculpins scoot across the bottom in much that fashion. And apart from nymph fishers imitating natural organisms, there is the entire spectrum of attractor nymphing, which relies on lively materials, flash, and erratic movement rather than precise imitation to attract attention and trigger strikes. In true prospecting—searching the water for scattered trout—I spend a lot more time attractor nymphing than I do precisely imitating natural nymphs.

WEIGHTING THE TIPPET

Nymphing in current with a floating line, weighted tippet, and unweighted or lightly weighted nymph has some inherent advantages. A small-diameter tippet weighted with split shot knifes through current, dropping the nymph quite vertically. Yet the unweighted nymph is free to buoy just off the bottom throughout the drift.

Since weighted tippets are much smaller in diameter than sinking fly lines, they're much less susceptible to drag. The combination of a floating fly line and weighted tippet also allows the use of a strike indicator on the leader, which telegraphs strikes and provides visual feedback during the drift, informing you at a glance whether your nymph is drifting naturally or beginning to drag. A floating fly line sitting on the surface is easily mended to counteract drag as you detect it.

Sinking fly lines and weighted flies are fixed in weight, but you can readily alter the amount of weight on your tippet as you progress along a stream through varying current speeds and depths. Having the flexibility to sink the nymph at the desired rate and to the desired depth as you move through a mix of water types is a big card to play, so play it liberally. Alter your shot arrangement as often as necessary. Taking a little time to fine-tune your sink rate to the depth and current speed is much more productive than fishing for prolonged periods with ineffective weight.

APPLYING SPLIT SHOT

Altering your shot arrangement is quick and easy if you streamline the process. Begin by discarding the compartmentalized boxes that split-shot assortments are sold in. Selecting shot from individual compartments is tedious, and those cheap rotating lids are prone to opening on their own, resulting in spillage. More than once I've dumped an entire compartment of shot into the water or grass as I removed a rotary shot box from a pocket. For years I've carried a full assortment of shot sizes in a breath mint container. I simply pop open the secure lid, shake a dozen or so shot into my palm, select those I want, and dump the remainder back into the mouth of the container. Every few outings, I refill the container with the shot sizes that are running low. I periodically shake the container to mix the shot so that a range of sizes always dumps into my palm.

With a bit of practice, applying shot to the tippet is simple. As a right-hander, I hold a shot with the groove up between my left thumb and forefinger, the leader running through my lightly clenched left fist. After seating the tippet in the shot groove, I simply pull down on the tippet, securely pinching it between the same thumb and forefinger that hold the shot. Now I have the tippet fully seated in the groove and under tension so that it can't travel, and my right hand is free to pinch the shot closed with pliers or hemostat. I can easily hold a couple additional loose shot between my fourth fingertip and left palm as I operate the hemostat with my right hand. Sometime when you're not fishing, grab some tippet material, some shot, and your hemostat, and work out the mechanics of applying shot smoothly and efficiently. Really observe the small details as you refine your technique. Once you can apply shot quickly and smoothly, altering the arrangement frequently as you move through different water types becomes second nature.

Pinching shot too tightly can nick fine tippets. Hard shot has more bite to its edges, so identify and use shot that is fairly soft. After pinching a shot onto 4X or finer tippet, I slide it a couple inches and feel for nicks in the pinch-on zone. That saves some nymphs and occasionally a good fish.

I find it more efficient to group smaller shot rather than use a single large shot. Adding shot in increments lets me adjust my sink rate quickly and precisely as I move from run to run. For instance, if I'm rigged with sizes 4 and 6 shot and encounter an exceptionally fast or deep run, I may add a size BB shot to my string. As I move to more normal flows for that particular stream, I can simply remove the size BB shot to get back to my original weighting.

POSITIONING SHOT

I generally position shot or putty within 6 to 8 inches of the nymph. When the shot ticks bottom, the unweighted nymph rides in the productive zone just above. Also, when casting nymphs at long ranges with high line speeds, I get fewer tangles if I keep the weight close to the nymph.

Casting with high line speeds can cause split shot to slide on the tippet, usually toward the nymph. In my experience, shot grips best with the original pinch. Once a shot begins to slide on the tippet, pinching it repeatedly, even mashing it, rarely stabilizes it. It's usually less grief to simply replace a sliding shot.

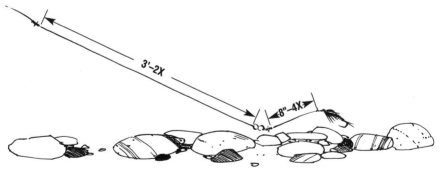

A compound tippet is abrasion-resistant and prevents shot from sliding toward the nymph during casting. A typical compound tippet for bouncing on the bottom is 3 to 4 feet of 2X with a short point section of 6 to 8 inches of 4X. The split shot goes on the 2X section just above the splicing knot. A split tippet in a single diameter, such as 3 feet of 3X with a short point section of 8 inches of 3X, also stabilizes split shot when casting at high line speeds.

You can avoid the problem of shot sliding toward the nymph by using a split tippet with a short point section of only 6 to 8 inches, and affixing shot just above the splicing knot. When I'm prospecting with big nymphs on 3X or stronger tippets and casting with lots of energy, I often do just that. For example, I might split my 3X tippet into an upper section of 20 inches and a short point section of 6 to 8 inches, and run my shot just above the adjoining blood knot.

A compound tippet also prevents shot from sliding toward the nymph and is a very efficient and abrasion-resistant rig for extended dead drifts over rock bottoms. You might run 3 feet of 2X tippet joined to a short point section of 8 inches of 4X tippet. Pinch enough shot to bounce on the bottom on the heavier 2X, which can take more abrasion. Tie an unweighted nymph to the short 4X point section; it will buoy naturally just off the bottom. Now you have a durable rig that is ideal for long drifts in direct contact with rocky bottoms.

REMOVING SHOT

Altering your shot arrangement regularly requires removing shot just as often as you add it. Most split shot used in fly fishing are too small to

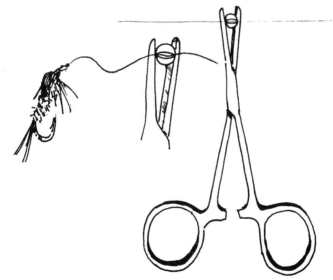

To remove round split shot, simply pull the tippet taut and squeeze the shot at a right angle to the tippet and shot groove. Even the smallest shot will usually open wide enough for easy removal. Keeping the tippet taut prevents it from being nicked as the shot is squeezed.

accommodate dog ears for easy removal. To easily remove small, round shot, stretch the tippet and shot over a forefinger, with the groove facing your finger. Lay the jaws of the hemostat against your fingertip at a right angle to the shot groove, and pinch the shot from the backside opposite the groove, flattening it a bit; it will usually open cleanly. If not, it at least will open enough to be spread and removed with a thumbnail. Keeping the tippet under good tension and pressed into your finger pad prevents it from being nicked as you flatten the shot. Since a split shot rarely grips well after its first use, I discard all used shot, including those that are not seriously deformed during removal.

CHECKING FOR LEADER FATIGUE

Nymphing subjects leaders and tippets to more abrasion than does fishing on top. Simply casting with weight on the leader accelerates tippet and knot fatigue. Get into the habit of quickly checking the integrity of your leaders as you're adding or removing shot. Slide the leader between a thumb and forefinger to feel for fraying or wind knots. If you feel any fraying of the tippet or the transition sections leading into the tippet, replace them.

Use the bounce test to check overall leader strength. Pinch the hook bend in your fingers or with your hemostat, then grab the middle of the leader with your opposite hand. Now quickly pull the leader taut a few times, exerting enough pressure to feel the leader sections bounce or stretch a bit. If you can feel some bounce and nothing gives, then your knots and tippet material are close to full strength. If your leader parts like cobweb in your hands, as it will on occasion, that's a good place to have it happen.

Use the "bounce test" to test the overall strength of your tippet and the transition sections just above it. Pinch the hook bend in your fingers or with pliers, and grab the leader a few feet above the fly. Pull the leader taut a few times, exerting enough pressure to feel the leader stretch or bounce a bit. If nothing gives, then your knots and tippet material are close to full strength.

ALTERNATIVE WEIGHTS

Lead sinkers are already illegal in Yellowstone Park and in a few states, and the list of areas where lead is prohibited is likely to grow. As a result, each year we're seeing more alternatives to lead split shot.

Most nontoxic split shot are tin alloy, which, like lead, is reasonably soft and inexpensive. Unfortunately, tin is significantly lighter than lead. To achieve the same sink rate as lead, a tin shot must be about 60 percent larger in diameter; that's an increase in mass of roughly 300 percent. When micronymphing, a tin shot of suitable weight is often larger than the nymph I'm fishing. Trout do strike weights, just as they strike indicators, and I prefer weight on the tippet to be as unobtrusive as possible.

Lead or nontoxic ribbon can be twisted around a tippet, but you need a long enough section to twist securely. Ribbon is difficult to apply in the small increments that I'm often looking to add.

Nontoxic weighted putty can be molded onto the tippet with your fingertips. It doesn't pinch or nick tippets, it stays positioned fairly well during casting, and it is reusable. These are all very nice properties. The putties I've used stiffen when exposed to cold air or water. It helps to carry the container where it absorbs body heat and to roll cold putty in your fingers to warm and soften it as you make weight adjustments, but I've found putties difficult to work with at cold temperatures. A putty as heavy as lead that remains pliable when cold would have a very attractive mix of properties.

Toobies Shot is an innovative system out of New Mexico (800-752-7132). A section of soft plastic tubing is slipped onto the tippet or leader, and a tool forces one or more nontoxic shot that are slightly heavier than lead into the tube. The shot are not grooved; they are held in position by friction between the tubing and tippet. The shot and tubing can be repositioned easily, and the smooth shot sleeve makes the system great for bouncing on the bottom with few hangups. Shot can be squeezed out of the tubing and reused indefinitely. The tool and shot are both magnetic for positive handling. Once you become proficient at handling the system, it has several clear advantages. Currently two kit sizes are sold; each kit includes two shot sizes (6 and 9, or 2 and 4) and two sizes of tubing.

From a performance and handling standpoint, I still like lead shot and frequently use it where it's legal and will not accumulate in significant quantities. Lead fishing shot are simply not the environmental hazard that lead shotgun pellets are. Compared with the ounce and a half of lead pellets per duck load, and the millions of duck loads that rained down annually over waterfowl marshes until about 1980, fishing shot is deposited in minute quantities and widely dispersed, usually at significant depths or over rocky substrates where waterfowl or other birds are extremely unlikely to ingest it. Be that as it may, lead is destined to be banned for more and more fishing. On the plus side, restricting the use of lead split shot should create a demand for high-quality nontoxic split shot that are comparable or superior to lead in density and softness. I'd gladly pay several times the price of lead split shot for a high-performance alternative.

LEADERS

Despite the many recent innovations in leader design and materials, I still build my own knotted leaders. Nymphing requires frequent rebuilding or altering of the leader, and with a knotted one, I know at a glance the diameter of every point on it. For speedy modification on the water without guesswork or the need to physically measure line diameters, knotted leaders are tops. By building your own leaders, you also work out butt and tippet formulas that perform well for you.

I do the majority of my trout fishing with 4- to 6-weight rods and with modifications to a single 8-foot 3X leader formula. I tie this leader in quantity and alter the length and tippet size right on the water to cover most of my trout fishing from top to bottom.

My basic 8-foot 3X leader formula:

40 inches of .017-inch (20-pound Maxima Chameleon)
14 inches of .015-inch (15-pound Maxima Chameleon)
8 inches of .012-inch (10-pound Maxima Chameleon)
8 inches of .011-inch (0X tippet material)
8 inches of .009-inch (2X tippet material)
20 inches of .008-inch (3X tippet material)

You can easily convert this to a 9-foot 4X leader by cutting the 3X section back to 10 inches and tacking on 20 inches of 4X tippet. You can convert that 4X leader to a 10-foot 5X leader by cutting the 4X back to 10 inches and tacking on about 20 inches of 5X, and so on. If you maintain a conventional tippet length of about 20 to 24 inches tacked to a 10-inch transition section, each 1X decrease in tippet diameter results in about 1 additional foot of leader length. This works well for most trout fishing from top to bottom, although I sometimes run 3- to 4-foot tippets off this leader formula. You can also convert the basic formula to 8-foot 2X or 1X by splicing 2 feet of 1X or 2X to the 0X transition section.

The stiffness of a leader butt is a function of length, diameter, and material. A leader butt that's considerably stiffer than the fly line doesn't turn over like an extension of the line during casting. A butt that's too limp doesn't transmit enough power to turn over weighted nymphs or tippets with authority and accuracy. I find that a 40-inch, .017-inch Chameleon leader butt is about right in stiffness for my general trout fishing with 4- to 6-weight lines.

Maxima Chameleon is available in convenient 27-yard spools for building leader butts. It is green and darker in shade than most tippet materials. As I modify my basic 3X formula, the third clear tippet section below the last green Chameleon section (the 8-inch, .012-inch section) is always 3X, so I know at a glance exactly where 3X is on the leader (and what tippet size I'm currently fishing one, two, or three sections below the 3X).

About half of my 40-inch leader butt is a 20-inch tag section of .017-inch Maxima that is spliced to my fly line with a needle knot, which is a nail knot tied after the butt is threaded through the tip of the fly line for about ¼ inch. With the leader butt extruding from the center of the fly line and the nail knot seated firmly into the line coating, there is no rough or bulky transition as the butt enters the rod guides. There is also no bulk or hinging between the fly line and the leader butt, so energy flows smoothly from the line into the leader. You don't want to have to tie a nail knot every time you change leaders, so tie on a permanent tag section, and then splice on your fresh leader with a blood knot. The permanent tag section loses about an inch each time you change leaders; as it grows shorter, you need to compensate by retaining more butt on the fresh leader in order to achieve a .017-inch butt that is 40 inches overall. If a tag gets too short or limp, change it. A change or two of tag sections covers the life of most fly lines.

Knotless leaders are often touted as far superior for fishing in weeds, moss, or scum. They're not. Junk picked up by knotless leaders simply slides down the leader and fouls the fly. Granted, knotted leaders are tougher to clean, because slime and moss catch on the individual knots, but nymphing in real slop is a pain with any leader design.

TIPPET LENGTH AND DIAMETER

Tippet length and diameter affect sink rate and drag coefficient. A 4X tippet sinks faster and creates less drag than a 3X tippet of the same length. It pays to remember, however, that increasing tippet length, rather than decreasing tippet diameter, also improves sink rate and decreases drag (while increasing, rather than decreasing, tippet strength). I often nymph with a 3-foot 3X tippet instead of a 2-foot 4X, or a 4-foot 4X tippet instead of a 3-foot 5X. Increasing tippet length, not decreasing the diameter, is usually my first choice when I need to increase my sink rate or reduce drag.

Many anglers forget that even within a given X size, tippet length affects tippet strength. A 3-foot 4X tippet has more stretch and strength than a 2-foot 4X. That can be critical when you're battling trout that are really taxing your tippet.

The water type I'm fishing always plays into my tippet construction. If I'm nymphing a small spring creek where I might need to check a 4-pound brown on a very short leash to keep it from powering under a nearby cutbank or downed tree, I often run a 3X tippet, or even 2X, and increase its length to 3 or 4 feet to help improve the sink rate and drift. If I'm fishing a small nymph on a big western river or an alpine lake where I can let a 4-pound trout run into my backing, I often go with a finer tippet, but I keep it long. Whenever I'm working to very strong trout, I like to lengthen my tippet for that extra shock absorbency.

As a rule, I like to cast the longest tippet I can turn with authority, given the nymph and shot arrangement I'm fishing. Casting significant weight into a strong headwind calls for a shorter tippet than casting with a tailwind or no wind. As I increase the weight of my rig, I often shorten my tippet to maintain casting accuracy. In long-line nymphing, turning weighted tippets over with authority is critical to casting accuracy. When my long-line nymphing accuracy isn't quite up to snuff, shortening the tippet just a few inches often puts my deliveries back on target.

TIPPET MATERIAL

There are many excellent tippet materials on the market. I've fished most of them and have never developed a runaway favorite. To me, condition is more critical than brand. I'd like to see the date of manufacture stamped right on the spools as standard procedure. Orvis is now putting an expiration sticker on their tippet spools, which serves much the same purpose. You can go into a busy fly shop that turns tippet material at a good clip and handpick spools with the latest expiration dates. At least you know you're not buying stuff that has sat on the shelf for an extended time. Over the years, I've canned a fair amount of 3X and lighter tippet, in both nylon and fluorocarbon, that had poor knot strength right off the shelf. I suspect age was the culprit. These days, I buy tippet with the latest expiration dates and don't buy more than one or two backup spools in 4X or finer, so that I'm always fishing reasonably fresh stuff in the small diameters. I keep backup tippet, spare fly lines, and camera film in a small accessory bag that I store in a relatively cool covered area of the vehicle so they don't slow-cook at 130 degrees. Bug dope is also bad news for tippets, fly lines, and many wader and rainwear fabrics and coatings; keep it off your palms to avoid transferring it to the equipment you handle.

Fluorocarbon tippet materials are touted to deliver higher knot strength, more abrasion resistance, a faster sink rate, and less visibility than nylon monofilaments—at about three times the cost. I have fished fluorocarbon with remarkable knot strength (I've completely straightened 2X heavy nymph hooks while pulling off snags with 3X tippet). Although abrasion resistance is higher, you still want to monitor fluorocarbon for fraying and replace damaged material. For nymphing, I discount the slightly faster sink rate of fluorocarbon; the amount of weight on the tippet or nymph remains the overriding factor. When submerged in a bowl of clear tap water, fluorocarbon essentially vanishes to my eyes, whereas I can still see nylon mono faintly. How many more strikes that translates into is tough to quantify. But overall, fluorocarbon has excellent nymphing properties, and I usually run it for my tippet and the transition section or two immediately above the tippet.

MULTIFLY RIGS

Although multifly nymphing rigs—either a nymph dropper below a dry fly or two- or three-nymphs—seem to be gaining in popularity, I fish them only occasionally. My nymphing style tends to be highly targeted and fast-paced: firing split shot with double-haul casts to specific stations; over-weighting my tippet for fast vertical sinks and short targeted drifts; actively moving the nymph much of the time; frequently altering my shot arrangement as I work a variety of presentation angles; casting sidearm and low to the water while long-line nymphing into stiff wind; delivering my forward cast into a hole in the foliage and my backcast to the water; casting over my off shoulder to lay the fly line tight to the far bank with a downstream bow and then actively employing drag to swim a soft-hackle nymph very seductively and parallel to the far bank; hugging a bank in brushy tunnels and using the downstream current to load my rod for casting. Given their complexity and penchant for tangling, multifly rigs are poorly suited for aggressive casting and difficult presentations. They work against flexibility and precision in nymphing in too many ways for my general liking, so I don't fish them much.

STRIKE INDICATORS

Strike indicators perform three important functions: They telegraph strikes and drag and can be used to suspend nymphs at controlled depths. Without question, indicators transmit many subtle takes of dead-drifting nymphs that would otherwise go undetected. The indicator provides a fixed point on the leader to focus on during the drift as you watch for an upstream dart, sudden pull beneath the surface, or light wobble. The take of a slow-drifting nymph by a stationary trout that merely intercepts the nymph is often very subtle, with the fish quickly expelling the artificial if the hook is not set immediately. For a dead-drift hookup, you generally have to detect the take quickly and set the hook promptly, and watching an indicator is frequently the best way to accomplish that.

When I'm fishing a nymph actively on a tight line, I often rely on detecting takes by feel, watching the zone around the nymph for the flash of a turning trout, or keeping an eye on the surface for the bulge of a charging fish. When dead drifting nymphs to visible trout, I often watch the fish instead of the indicator for a quick lateral shift, downward tip, or white flash of mouth that signals a take. But for conventional dead-drift nymphing to unseen trout, a strike indicator is invaluable, even for very experienced anglers.

In dead-drift nymphing, if you can present the indicator without drag, then the nymph also drifts without drag. And fishing an indicator without drag is very much like fishing a dry fly without drag; many of the same slack-line casts, reach casts, and mends can be used to keep the indicator—and the nymph below it—drifting freely.

A buoyant indicator can be used to suspend a nymph at a controlled depth throughout a drift. I often run enough shot on the tippet to suspend a tiny micronymph vertically beneath the indicator. Using a buoyant indicator and weight on the tippet allows you to present a nymph at a fixed depth over a very long drift, even on very slow runs, without ever fouling on weeds or bottom. I frequently make subtle depth adjustments of the indicator to put the nymph within inches of the bottom at the precise level of podded trout, and many times this winds up generating a flurry of strikes from a compact zone.

Many of the same fly fishers who denounce the use of split shot dismiss strike indicators as nothing more than fly-fishing bobbers. It's true that indicators aid in strike detection and can be used to suspend nymphs at controlled depths, but I still find indicator fishing to be quite technique intensive and absorbing, not to mention productive. The downside of defining fly fishing too narrowly is that you wind up on the water an awful lot of the time without the inclination, tools, or skills to adjust. Many days, especially on hard-fished public waters, you need to get down and dirty, make adjustments, and be resourceful to hook nice trout consistently or have a legitimate shot at sticking those few top-end fish. I enjoy matching hatches, and I enjoy prospecting with a dry fly when it's effective. But there's nothing appealing to me about fishing over the top of the better trout with almost no chance of bringing them up. Fly fishers who object to split shot and indicators can have my share of that kind of fishing.

Since indicators perform several functions, you should carry several styles. For active nymphing, I usually run a strike putty indicator high on the leader butt; with the nymph hung in the hook keeper of the rod, I position the putty about a foot from the tip guide. When I'm fishing a nymph actively on a tight line, I detect many strikes by feel or sight; the indicator is primarily a supplement to monitor when I'm dead drifting or moving the nymph very slowly. When I'm fishing a nymph actively and am not primarily dependent on the indicator for detecting strikes, I find that running a putty indicator high on the leader butt has several major advantages. As I nymph through various depths, my nymph is free to plummet to the bottom, even in the deeper pockets (when I'm fishing the nymph actively, I usually don't want the indicator regulating fly depth or impeding the drop of the nymph). When I need to reach out with a long cast, my line speed, leader turnover, and accuracy are all improved by running the indicator high on the butt, especially a putty indicator that can be rolled and tapered to minimize air resistance. Bopping—dropping the indicator directly on top of shallow fish—is reduced by moving the indicator up the leader.

Nymphing often requires working in close contact with the bottom, which can result in frequent hangups, but running a putty indicator high on the butt allows me to salvage many nymphs and tippets. Here's the procedure: When I hang up on the bottom, I reel the line tight as I wade close to

With the nymph hung in the reel frame, the tip of the fly line is just outside the tip guide, which prevents kinking of the leader butt. A leader that's just slightly shorter than the rod generally delivers positive turnover and excellent accuracy when casting weighted rigs. A putty indicator is high on the leader butt. Split shot are about 8 inches above the nymph.

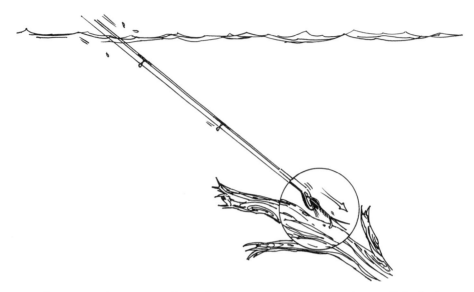

When a nymph snags securely on the bottom, strip the putty indicator off the leader butt, crank the rod tip right down to the nymph, and gently back the nymph off the obstruction with rod tip pressure. This technique salvages the majority of badly snagged nymphs, which allows you to work the bottom and structure more aggressively.

my nymph. With the putty positioned high on the butt, I can usually reach it with a hand and strip it. After stripping the indicator, I submerge the rod tip toward the nymph and continue reeling until I feel my split shot pass through the tip guide, which tells me the tip is only inches from the nymph. Then I gently snug the rod tip right down to the nymph and use light tip pressure to back the hook off rock or out of wood. Stripping and reapplying a putty indicator is much faster and less annoying than breaking off nymphs unnecessarily in flows and depths that are perfectly wadable. More importantly, having the capability to salvage the majority of snagged nymphs frees me to aggressively pound that productive bottom zone. I've never damaged a rod tip or lost a rod section, but if you use this salvage technique, make sure your sections are firmly seated; if your rod comes apart and you wind up breaking the leader, you could lose more than your nymph.

At cold temperatures, putty can stiffen and fall off. After extended casting, a putty indicator develops dog ears that can grab the tippet in flight. Periodically reshaping the putty cures both problems.

A putty indicator is easily sized up or down to increase or decrease its visibility. When I want an indicator that is drab and unobtrusive, and not alarming to spooky trout, I tone down a small hunk of putty by working silt into it with my fingers.

As indicators go, putty is not particularly buoyant. I actually consider that an advantage for general prospecting with substantial attractor nymphs. When I encounter a particularly deep run or pocket, I want the weighted rig to pull the indicator beneath the surface so that the nymph can plummet freely into the depths. On very deep presentations—both dead drifts and active strips—I detect a lot of strikes by watching a putty indicator that is submerged but still visible.

The buoyancy of a putty indicator is easily boosted by increasing its size. When I'm running a small putty indicator high on the leader butt and encounter a run where I want to suspend the nymph at a controlled depth, I often reposition the putty lower on the leader and make it larger to increase buoyancy.

But putty is rarely my first choice for suspending nymphs at controlled depths. To do this, I prefer Palsa pinch-on foam indicators. For their small size, these soft, microcell foam indicators are exceptionally buoyant. I particularly favor them for micronymphing. I typically rig with just enough small shot to suspend a tiny nymph directly beneath the indicator, and I fine-tune my indicator position to present the nymph at the exact level of the fish, usually just inches above bottom. A Palsa indicator sits so high and perky on the water that it actually wobbles slightly to telegraph the most subtle, slow-speed take (its flat bottom profile and high float accentuate the wobble).

An inherent drawback of adhesive indicators is that their grip on the leader fails pretty quickly as you reposition them. I solve that problem by not relying on the adhesive. To rig a Palsa indicator, I pinch it shut, poke a hole through the middle from top to bottom, thread it onto the leader, and lock it in position with a short section of flat toothpick. That gives me the ability to reposition the indicator at will and reuse it indefinitely. For vertical presentations over shallow trout, I tone down some of my Palsa indicators by shading the bottom and sides with a drab permanent marker. I shade, pinch shut, perforate, and fit Palsa indicators with toothpick stoppers in advance of fishing so they are ready for use.

The huge yarn indicators, popular with driftboat guides in the West, are easily tracked by everyone in the boat, including the guide, and can suspend even heavily weighted rigs. If you need to suspend a heavy rig and don't have an outsize indicator, you can combine two or more foam indicators to boost buoyancy. Likewise, in low light or harsh glare, you can string small indicators together to increase visibility.

LINE TAPERS

I use weight-forward lines for all my nymphing. For nymphing lakes, where the casting is often quite long, these lines are a major advantage. Even on moving water, I often shoot well into the thin belly section of a weight-forward line on long-line nymphing deliveries.

If you've tangled with hot-running stillwater trout on fairly light tippets, then you also appreciate the fighting advantages of weight-forward lines. An entire double-taper fly line being towed at high speeds in a deep bow generates enough drag to pop a 4X tippet. Where trout have the power to zip into your backing and the running room to tow an entire fly line in a wide arc, you want a fly line with a thin belly, not a fat one.

ROD CHOICE

For slinging shot, I like a rod with medium flex that loads fairly easily into the butt but doesn't collapse when I punch it for extra speed and distance on the delivery. As you become proficient at slinging shot, you can readily adjust to most rod actions, but some rods definitely load and unload more smoothly into their butts with weighted payloads, and smoothing out your delivery is a key to minimizing miscues and tangles with weighted rigs.

I do the majority of my nymphing for trout with 4- to 6-weight rods. Water type, fly size and weight, wind speed, and casting distance dictate the rod that I grab for a given session.

For presenting small to medium nymphs on small streams, I usually throw an 8-foot 4-weight. I have quite a few 4-weights in my arsenal, but the shorter rods invariably have smaller-diameter butts than the longer rods, so they load more easily into their butts with just 10 to 20 feet of line outside the rod tip. That translates into higher line speeds and better accuracy at short to medium ranges—and small-stream nymphing often places a premium on accuracy inside of 40 feet.

I will break out a 9-foot 5-weight rod on fairly small spring creeks if it's windy, or if the creek is open enough that I'm regularly throwing sizable nymphs or streamers for 40-plus feet. A 9-foot 5-weight will deliver a weighted nymph fairly easily at ranges and in winds that can be considerable work with shorter, lighter rods.

For sizable streams and rivers, I usually nymph with a 9-foot 4-weight or 9-foot 5-weight. If I anticipate mixing in quite a bit of dry-fly fishing or primarily casting micronymphs, I often grab the 4-weight. If I plan to toss mostly sizable nymphs or streamers, I usually grab the 5-weight.

For lakes, I primarily fish a 9-foot 6-weight. Lakes tend to be windy places, and the casting is usually on the long side, calling for a trout rod that's a bit on the power end of the spectrum.

For casting air-resistant streamers and sinking lines, I'll use a 7-weight or heavier rod, but I rarely have occasion to nymph trout with rods that heavy.

CHAPTER 2

Casting Weighted Rigs

Forget everything you've heard about lobbing weighted nymphs, chucking and ducking, and the general grousing surrounding the aesthetics of casting weighted rigs. Fly-casting with weight on the fly or tippet, whether it's a little weight or a lot, is a precise and enjoyable skill, and essential for unlocking some of the most potent and engaging forms of nymphing.

Delivering a weighted payload with near dry-fly accuracy, especially at moderate to long ranges of 40 to 70 feet, requires significant line speed and a refined two-part casting stroke that includes an energized backcast and a smooth application of power on the forward cast. Lobbing doesn't describe it. I often haul on the backcast to straighten a weighted rig with authority. And I often haul on the forward cast to help generate the line speed needed to turn over weighted rigs crisply and accurately.

As for aesthetics, once you get the basic stroke and timing down, casting weighted rigs—or "slinging shot," as I often call it—is actually a relaxing and pleasurable form of fly casting that deviates very little from fundamentally sound dry-fly casting. You feel a well-executed backcast straightening with sufficient energy. And on delivery, you feel the rod loading right into the butt and then smoothly unloading as you sling the weighted payload. As you develop a smooth acceleration of power on the forward cast off of a fully extended backcast, surprising accuracy and distance follow. The ability to sling shot with controlled loops and significant line speed greatly improves accuracy at standard nymphing ranges, even into stiff winds, and it opens doors to more distant and targeted forms of nymphing.

The similarity between casting dry flies and slinging weighted payloads is a good-news, bad-news scenario. If your dry-fly casting is fundamentally sound, you'll have little trouble making the transition to slinging shot or weighted nymphs with real authority. Conversely, if you encounter major difficulty in learning to sling weight with speed and precision, it's because your fly casting, including your dry-fly casting, has some fundamental issues. Back to the good news: The overhead cast that is the foundation for casting weighted rigs is the foundation for most fly casting. As you absorb the fundamentals and fine points of slinging shot with the overhead cast, your dry-fly casting will also benefit.

PRACTICE TIPS AND INCENTIVES

You can do a lot in the backyard to develop your dry-fly casting. Not so with slinging shot, which is a less aerial form of casting. In its most efficient form, slinging shot or weighted nymphs involves coming off the water with sufficient energy to load the rod with a single backcast and then getting the nymph right back into the water. False casting can be minimized or eliminated, even when throwing weighted payloads for substantial distances, but you need the resistance of water to help load the rod smoothly and accelerate the line and weighted rig on your initial backcast. You can learn the fundamentals of slinging shot by practicing on standing water, but eventually you need to practice on moving water to learn to accelerate your backcast with various pickups and line lengths as you're coming off of actual drifts.

Initially, you'll advance more quickly if you separate your casting practice from your fishing for at least a few sessions, while you focus entirely on the mechanics and timing of slinging shot. Once you have the basic stroke, then you can begin refining and diversifying your deliveries and pickups in the course of your fishing. Even after years of slinging shot, however, I still take time out from fishing to work on the mechanics of casting weighted rigs and really concentrate on the fine points of what I'm doing, particularly with my casting hand.

What you do with your casting hand transmits through the rod to the line, and small flaws in hand movement are greatly amplified 30, 50, or 70 feet out at the point of the fly. From time to time, observe the path of your casting hand and how each small movement influences the path of the rod tip and the flight of the line for good or bad. Observing the movement of your hand, the path of the rod tip, and the resulting path of the line can help you weed out some negative influences. If you turn to look at your backcast, don't twist your torso; that throws your casting hand and arm out of their normal alignment. Make the backcast first, then turn your head to peek over your shoulder at the line.

In my prospecting, I often cast with substantial shot on the tippet for most of the day, covering several miles of stream and firing casts at hundreds of different lies, often on overgrown streams on windy days. If you commit to slinging weighted rigs regularly in your practice and fishing, you'll soon be making casts that most others aren't up to making and working water that most fly fishers routinely avoid. On my home spring creeks in southwestern Wisconsin, I find that most anglers flock to a handful of open and inviting ones. They're simply not up to casting weighted rigs, or even dry flies, on the more obstructed streams where they could enjoy fine fishing in solitude.

Even on wide open creeks where casting lanes are completely unobstructed, few anglers can deliver weighted nymphs with real precision at even 20 or 30 feet. At modest ranges, it still takes decent line speed and crisp turnover to deliver weighted nymphs precisely, and most anglers simply have not honed their shot-casting techniques. That's a mistake, because small creeks in particular often demand precise and creative nymphing on run after run.

Picture a sparkling little spring creek riffle that is only 3 feet wide, with overhanging grass guarding a cutbank that a trout can tuck under. Say your casting distance to the cutbank hideout is a mere 20 feet, but you're a right-handed caster standing on the left bank, and the cutbank is on the other side of the stream. To angle your cast upstream into the right bank with enough slack piled into the leader that the current grabs your nymph instantly and sweeps it under the grass and cutbank, you need to deliver a tuck cast from the left bank over your left shoulder. And you need to deposit the nymph right on the edge of the grass. Now let's add a brisk headwind and make that trout hiding under the cutbank a mature brown, the kind of trout that you nail on the first presentation or he's wise to you. Suddenly that short, 20-foot cast is plenty challenging. The reality is that even user-friendly creeks require precise and creative short-range casting on run after run if you're going to consistently nymph the trickier trout that other anglers are bypassing or bungling.

And small-stream nymphing is by no means limited to short-range casting. I fish small spring creeks more than any other water type, and most of them have long, glassy slicks where inactive trout really stack up. Putting the sneak on a pod of nervous small-stream trout sulking on bottom on a wide open flat can be impossible. Often the solution is a weighted nymph air mailed from beyond radar range of the trout.

The ability to deliver weighted payloads with precision at 40, 50, or 60 feet allows you to dispense with tedious stalking in many situations. That in turn allows you to pick up your pace and cover water at a much more efficient clip. Stealth and patience have their place, but longer, more precise casting and a faster pace will often trump them. Doubling or tripling the amount of water you prospect very often doubles or triples your number of hookups, especially when trout are highly active and primed to whack a nymph on the first presentation. Of course, nymphing along fine and far at a fast clip, or any highly targeted form of nymphing, hinges on being able to cast weighted rigs with significant line speed and real accuracy.

Big rivers can often be nymphed more efficiently if you can fire weighted rigs 60 feet or more to probe distant current seams and far banks. Also, big rivers with their powerful flows often call for slinging considerable weight to sink the nymph. But nymphing on big rivers doesn't always call for casting 60 feet of fly line and a heavy shot string. When big-river trout are highly active, they often move out of deep refuge areas into shallow riffles, pockets, weed channels, and banks, where they can be nymphed at short to moderate ranges with the same precise and creative casts employed on small creeks.

My favorite lake fishing is backpacking wilderness areas and sight-casting to cruising trout in high mountain lakes. As with most sight fishing, when an eye-popping golden or brook trout ghosts into view, you may need to fire a weighted nymph 70-plus feet with minimal false casting and sink the fly into the path of a fast-moving fish before it disappears. Since high lakes with trophy trout often have low fish densities, you may get only a few fleeting opportunities at big cruisers, even on a good day. Seventy miles of hiking with a 60-pound pack and three days of prowling an alpine lake can all boil down to what you do with a few critical casts with a weighted nymph.

Creeks, rivers, spring ponds, lakes—there's not a water type where being able to sling split shot or weighted nymphs for accuracy and distance won't play to your advantage. Yet when is the last time you saw a fly fisher practice slinging shot? Or read something about casting weighted nymphs precisely? Or bumped into somebody out on the water who was smoothly double-hauling a heavy shot string, shooting line, and delivering casts right on the money?

Casting weighted rigs may be the most neglected major skill in fly fishing. And I do mean major, considering the many payoffs for doing it well. The perplexing thing is that casting weight with precision and speed requires only a few adjustments in timing and stroke. In fact, as I work with other anglers on zinging weighted rigs and it begins to click for them, many are a bit annoyed at how effortless it turns out to be, after years of buying into the flawed notion that they should be lobbing weighted rigs with big, slow, unfocused loops.

Grasp the fundamentals, get out and practice, and slinging shot and weighted nymphs will begin to click for you. Then put your practice to work regularly in your fishing, and you'll see rapid development in your distance and accuracy using a wide range of deliveries.

Casting is a highly technical subject. Not everything you read here will soak in on the first pass, or even the second. Read, cast, read again, and cast again until you have absorbed sound fundamentals and applied them to your casting. As you read, you can benefit by performing the casting movements while holding just the butt section of a rod or extending your index finger as a rod substitute. Forming fundamentally sound casting movements may require breaking a few old habits, which is often easier to do without actually casting, because you can focus specifically on cleaning up your movements without worrying about results. Once your movements are on track, positive results will follow.

A word about safety: An eye is the one thing on your person that a speeding fly hook or split shot can do lasting damage to. Whenever you fly cast, whether it's fishing or practice, wear glasses or sunglasses to protect your eyes. As you're first learning to cast weighted rigs with significant line speeds, it's not a bad idea to snip the entire hook point from your nymph. Without that point, you're free to push your limits in practice without paying a painful price if a weighted payload bounces out of control.

GRIP

Dropping the backcast is probably the most common major casting flaw, and a floppy wrist is the usual culprit. Flopping the wrist causes the rod tip to arc throughout the entire stroke, like the sweeping hand of a clock, dropping the backcast too low. This can be especially painful when casting a weighted rig, which is likely to whack you from behind if it is free-falling as you begin the forward cast (hence the "duck" in "chuck-and-duck"). Excessive arcing also blows your line loops wide open, robbing your casts of energy and control. Extending the index finger along the grip firms up the wrist, making it difficult to flop the wrist too far back on the backcast. Try doing this if excessive arcing of the rod tip is a problem.

I've always cast with my index finger extended because it's always been my most accurate grip. On delivery, my finger points at the target and the fly naturally follows. As a right-handed caster, my extended index finger rests near the top of the cork grip—not directly on top, but at about the one o'clock position. Only the pad of the finger contacts the cork; the remainder of the finger is fairly straight but elevated off the grip. Elevating the finger a bit is more relaxing than flattening it against the cork. Also,

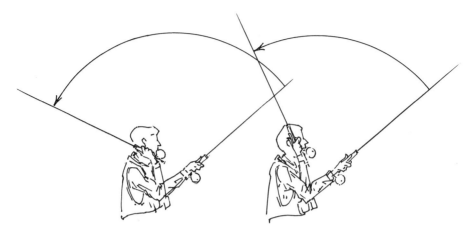

With the thumb-on-top grip, it's easy to flop the wrist and the rod too far back on the backcast, resulting in excessive arcing of the rod tip and a host of related casting problems (left). Extending the index finger along the grip makes it physically diffi-cult to flop the wrist too far back (right), resulting in a high, well-extended backcast that sets up smooth, high-speed delivery of a weighted rig on the forward cast.

having just the front pad in contact with the grip provides a very controlled pressure point that translates into finer accuracy. During the forward cast, fine-tuning of pressure from the index finger enhances accuracy. This is a difficult thing to describe but an easy thing to feel once it begins to happen for you.

Compared with the thumb-on-top grip, with all four fingers wrapped underneath, extending the index finger lengthens the grip by a third, significantly increasing sensitivity and control. Much of the flexing or loading you feel when the rod loads and unloads into the butt is through that elongated grip and your extended finger.

It becomes natural to maintain this grip all the time and extend your middle finger for line pickup and pinching. This gains you a good half inch of reach, making it easier to transfer the line to your pinch finger while the cast is still in the air. That pays off when an aggressive fish charges and nails the nymph on impact, which is a frequent occurrence when nymphing to active trout on relatively shallow feeding stations. Transferring the line to your pinch finger while it's airborne also allows you to begin stripping or moving the fly immediately on impact. That's an advantage when you are nymphing straight upstream in very fast water or want to strip a weighted nymph just subsurface on smooth water to create an attention-

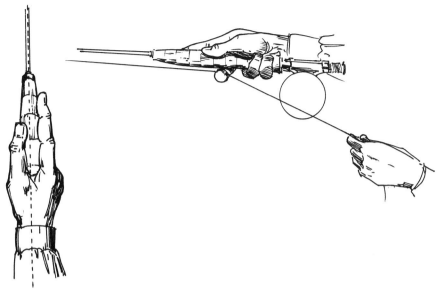

Extending the index finger along the grip has many advantages. Note the excellent alignment of forearm, wrist, hand, and rod. Throughout the cast, the rod and the index finger point in almost the same direction. Consequently, you develop an awareness of how far the rod is dropping on the backcast, and your index finger points right at the target on the forward cast. Using the middle finger for line pickup allows you to maintain a consistent grip for casting and stripping. The extended reach provided by the middle finger allows easy transfer of the line to the "pinch" finger before the nymph hits the water on the delivery cast.

grabbing wake, a technique I frequently employ on lakes and smooth stream flats.

If you cast with your index finger extended and then move it under the grip for line handling, your hand must shift considerably on the grip as you go from casting to stripping and back to the casting position. But if your index finger remains in the casting position while you use your middle finger for line control, your grip stays consistent, increasing your casting control.

Whatever grip you use, the heel of your hand should stay on top of the rod. Keeping the heel of your hand on top aligns the rod with your forearm; letting the heel of your hand slide off the grip creates a basic misalignment between the rod and your arm, which can have all kinds of negative consequences.

LINE-HAND POSITION

As you begin to work on developing a controlled overhead cast with a weighted rig, I suggest that you cast a fixed length of line and take your line hand out of the cast. Simply pinch the line against the grip with your rod hand as you cast. This accomplishes two important things: First, you maintain a tight fly line, so the rod begins to load immediately during the backcast and the forward cast. And second, you avoid an array of casting problems caused by imprecise use of the line hand.

I see many casters with a lackadaisical line hand widely separated from the rod hand throughout the cast. In extreme cases, the line hand dangles around the waist as the rod hand reaches the top of the backcast. As the forward cast begins, and the rod hand starts forward and down, the 3-plus feet of fly line that has developed between the line hand and stripping guide goes slack. As the forward cast proceeds, instead of the rod loading against a well-tensioned backcast, slack feeds up through the guides, robbing the rod of a tight line to load against. This kills energy transfer and is the antithesis of hauling, which shortens (not lengthens) the line during the cast to accelerate the line for long-distance deliveries, or for bucking wind, or simply for more efficient casting. And a low, lazy line hand is the primary cause of slippage.

Once your overhead casting is sound, then add your line hand back into the cast, but do it productively. Ideally, the line hand should stay within about a foot of your rod hand and mirror its movements. For casting at short to moderate ranges, it's not necessary for the line hand to mirror rod-hand movements precisely, but keep your hands close enough together that significant slack doesn't develop between them. At the top of the backcast, the line hand should be fairly close to your chin, not dangling around your waist. That ensures that as the forward cast begins, your rod encounters line tension and loading forces immediately, particularly important for casting weighted rigs smoothly. Keeping your rod hand close to your line hand also sets you up for hauling.

When starting out, I suggest that you also eliminate false casting. Simply pick up a fixed length of line and put it back down on the water. That distills the overhead cast down to its essential movements and conditions you to minimize false casting in your nymphing.

THE OVERHEAD BACKCAST

Where there are no overhead obstructions, an overhead cast with a moderately open loop is all you need to sling weighted nymphs without fouling and with real accuracy at typical nymphing distances of 20 to 40 feet. Once

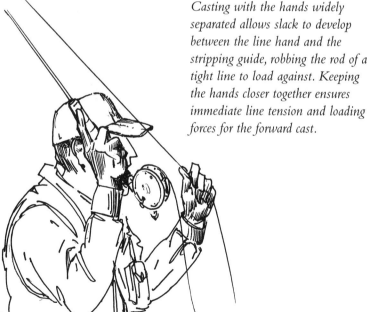

Casting with the hands widely separated allows slack to develop between the line hand and the stripping guide, robbing the rod of a tight line to load against. Keeping the hands closer together ensures immediate line tension and loading forces for the forward cast.

you're slinging shot crisply with this basic cast, it's quite easy to tilt the rod plane from vertical (overhead) all the way down to horizontal (sidearm) to cast around obstructions and improve your presentation angles. And once you can perform a crisp overhead cast with weighted rigs on a fixed length of line, you're set to incorporate hauling and shooting to increase your line speed and casting distance.

The first important element in slinging shot with authority is straightening the backcast with sufficient speed and loft. With the line, leader, and weighted payload extending back and up on the backcast, not dropping or driven toward the water behind you, you're in perfect position to accelerate smoothly into the forward cast.

If you fail to straighten the backcast, the rod has little line weight to load against on the forward cast. The result is much the same as pedaling a bicycle with the back wheel off the ground. You can pedal like mad, but you're not going anywhere. Likewise, you can muscle up on the forward cast until the veins pop out on your forehead, but if the backcast is not extended when you begin the forward cast, you'll be throwing without appreciable line weight to load the rod, and your deliveries will be anemic.

Failing to impart sufficient energy to straighten the backcast is particularly common when casting weighted rigs; it takes a bit more power and a

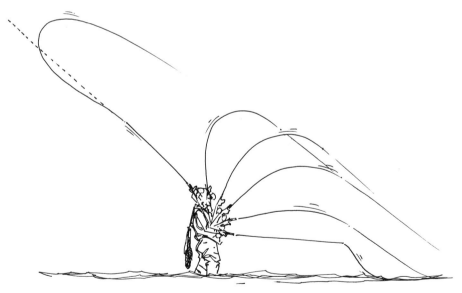

A complete initial overhead backcast, including the lift off the water. Note that the rod stops at a bit past vertical and the cast extends back and up. As the line straightens, you're in perfect position to accelerate smoothly into the forward cast.

slightly longer, smoother application of power to straighten the backcast with a weighted rig. Starting the forward cast too soon, before the backcast has an opportunity to fully straighten, is another extremely common error when casting weighted rigs; it takes a bit longer for a sinking rig to be lifted out of the water and extended behind you.

To develop and practice good extension and loft on your overhead backcast, rig a rod and get out on the water. I suggest rigging with a floating line, an 8-foot 3X leader, an indicator high on the leader butt, a lightly weighted nymph in about size 12, and a pair of medium split shot in size 4 or 6. Being on water is almost mandatory; split shot and weighted nymphs do not lift cleanly off grass, and you want the steady resistance of the water on the fly line to help load the rod smoothly right from the initial stages of the pickup.

Lay about three rod lengths (about 30 feet) of line and leader on the water. Make sure that the line is extended straight on the water in front of you so that the rod begins to load immediately during the initial lifting phase of the backcast. The ideal setup is facing downstream on moderate current that will automatically straighten your fly line.

Keep everything simple at first. Work with a fixed length of line, and take your line hand out of the picture for now; just pinch the line tight against the rod grip with a finger of your rod hand. Don't false-cast. Work on achieving good extension and loft on your backcast with your initial pickup off the water. Don't worry about making the forward cast until you're consistently achieving good extension and loft on the backcast. After each backcast, get the line extended on the water in front of you any old way: by roll-casting, using the downstream current, or lobbing it out there. The method isn't important for now; what is important is that the line is straight on the water so that the rod begins to load smoothly as soon as you start the backcast.

During the initial lifting stage of the backcast, slowly lift the rod tip and slide the line toward you on the water until the line tip is moving, then accelerate into your pickup and backcast. Getting the very tip of the line moving takes away any slack and helps the fly line break the water tension smoothly. If you try to snatch a stationary or slack line off the water, your weighted rig will bounce wildly out of control as the line breaks water tension too suddenly and snaps tight on the pickup. When backcasting a weighted rig, try extending your rod hand forward a bit farther than normal at the start of the lift; that allows a longer, smoother acceleration of power into the backcast, which helps you generate more line speed without herky-jerky loss of control.

There's that S word again—*smooth*. Casting a weighted rig is like driving a car with a gallon jug of milk sitting unsupported on the front floorboard. You can still hit or exceed the speed limit, but if you accelerate too sharply, especially from a dead stop, that milk jug is going to bounce around. Likewise, although you can still generate high line speeds, if you accelerate too sharply on the backcast or forward cast, a weighted nymph rig is going to bounce out of control.

Take any cast you can do with a dry fly, from the double haul to the steeple cast, and think in terms of longer, smoother acceleration, and you are well on your way to duplicating that cast, in both distance and accuracy, with a weighted rig. But if you get herky-jerky with your acceleration, you will likely pay with a thoroughly rat-nested rig or a bug in the back of the head. Weighted rigs are very unforgiving of misapplications of power; once energized in the wrong direction, they have a weight and momentum of their own that makes them difficult to rein in. To stay in control, keep all slack out of your casts and apply power smoothly over a slightly longer stroke than you'd use to cast an unweighted fly the same distance.

There's another inherent advantage to casting weighted rigs with longer strokes: Short strokes tend to load mainly the tip of the fly rod, but longer strokes load the rod deeper into the butt. Loading the rod deeper and more uniformly results in a longer, smoother release of energy on both the backcast and the forward cast, which feeds into the overall goal of accelerating weighted rigs smoothly.

A standard overhand backcast begins with your forearm nearly horizontal and your elbow tucked in close to your body. During the backcast, your rod hand moves upward and back in a fairly straight line, not in a sweeping arc. Envision your hand moving from two o'clock at the start of the backcast to eleven o'clock at the end of the backcast, except that your hand does not arc through the one and twelve o'clock positions. Instead, it shortcuts across the face of the clock directly from two to eleven. Up and back up on a straight line, and more upward than backward—that's the path of the hand on a standard overhead backcast. Practice that hand path from two to eleven, up and back on a straight line.

An overhead backcast of average distance ends with your rod hand at about ear level and close to your head, and the rod shaft tilted slightly past vertical. If you move your hand upward and back on a straight line and stop the rod just past vertical, the backcast will continue to extend upward and back (assuming you've imparted sufficient energy).

At the top of a standard overhead backcast, your elbow approaches shoulder height and your forearm is close to vertical. If the elbow swings

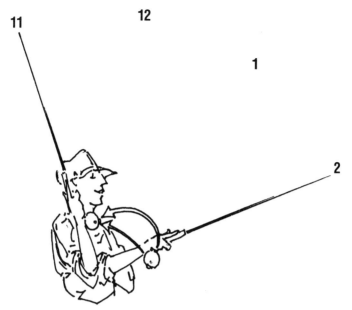

During the overhead backcast, the hand and the reel move upward and back in a straight line or slight arc, not in a large, sweeping arc. Envision your hand shortcutting across a clock face from two to eleven without sweeping through the one o'clock and twelve o'clock positions.

too high, the forearm is typically forced way past vertical, arcing the rod tip downward and dropping the backcast. The same thing happens if the wrist is flopped way open.

Flipping the wrist upward as you near the top of the backcast fully accelerates the rod and begins loop formation, but the wrist flip must be controlled, not floppy. Try aligning your hand and forearm as though you're going to make a karate chop, keeping your palm vertical. This karate-chop orientation does not change throughout the overhead cast; at any point, you should be able to turn your head and look directly into the palm of your rod hand. The wrist does not rotate outward on the backcast; the back of your hand never comes into view, not even if you sneak a peek at the top of the backcast. Unintentional wrist rotation is another major casting bugaboo. If the wrist rotates outward during the backcast and inward during the forward cast, the path of the rod tip will be curved and the line will curve right along with it, robbing your casts of forward energy and leading to unintended line crossovers and tangles.

To develop a controlled wrist flip, practice without the rod. Assume a karate-chop position, with your palm vertical. From the backcast start

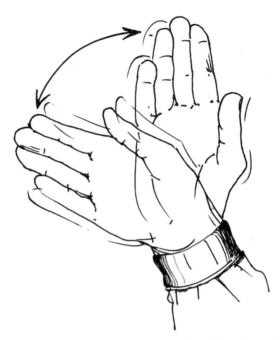

To develop a controlled wrist flip, orient your hand for a karate chop, then flip your wrist up and down as far as it will travel without moving your forearm. During the overhead backcast, your wrist will flip up as the rod approaches vertical. During the overhead forward cast, your wrist will flip down as your rod hand passes your face and enters your peripheral vision.

position, moving just your wrist, not your arm, flip your wrist up and then down as far as it will comfortably travel. You'll note that with your palm vertical, your wrist can be flipped easily through only a fairly limited range that approaches 90 degrees, which is about right for most fly casting.

Now return to the backcast start position and practice flipping your wrist as you will in an actual backcast. Starting with your forearm horizontal, lift and accelerate it to vertical, flipping your wrist upward as the forearm nears vertical. That's all there is to making a crisp overhead backcast with a weighted rig directly off the water. Lift to get the tip of the line gliding toward you. Accelerate your hand smoothly upward and back in a straight line from two o'clock to eleven o'clock. As your hand approaches head level, flip your wrist upward to fully accelerate the rod and begin loop formation. Stop the rod just a bit past vertical to transfer rod energy into the line and complete loop formation. And do it all—the lift, the acceleration into the wrist flip, and the stop—in one continuous motion.

Practice just the backcast with a fixed line length of about 30 feet until your backcast is extending nicely upward and back. Give your backcast time to straighten by developing a definite pause at the end before starting the forward cast. When your hand stops moving at the end of the backcast, the rod tip and line have not stopped moving. You need that definite pause to give the loaded rod time to unflex toward the rear and the energized line time to unroll and straighten behind you. If all goes well in your backcasting practice, you will feel a slight tug as the energized line, leader, and weighted terminal rig straighten completely. And ramrod straight is what you want on the overhead backcast.

By the time you feel that tug at the end of the backcast, the rod tip is actually rebounding forward and the backcast is beginning to drop toward the water, which you definitely don't want with a weighted rig. To avoid the pronounced bouncing of a weighted rig at the end of an energized backcast (and the resulting loss of line tension and control), after you've stopped the rod to transfer energy, allow your rod hand to drift slightly upward and back along the path of the backcast as the line straightens behind you. Any backward drift of the rod hand should occur only after the rod has been stopped and the energized backcast is already straightening. If you don't stop the rod on the backcast, you won't get full energy transfer from the rod into the line. To an observer, the rod stop and the slight drift appear almost seamless, but the rod stop does occur.

Slight rearward drift of the rod hand also sets up room for longer, smoother acceleration on the forward cast. A fully extended backcast with smooth acceleration on the forward cast is exactly what you want for slinging weighted rigs.

THE OVERHEAD FORWARD CAST

Once you have your overhead backcast extending nicely with a weighted rig, the overhead forward cast is a relative cinch. It follows much the same path but in reverse: The rod hand smoothly accelerates down and forward into a forward wrist flip, and the rod tip stops above the horizontal. As you work to develop a crisp overhead forward cast with a weighted rig, work with a fixed line length of about 30 feet. Keep your line hand out of the picture at first, just as you did in developing your backcast.

On an overhead forward cast of average distance, stop the rod about halfway between horizontal and vertical to transfer energy from the rod into the line in a forward direction. Powering the rod too far toward the water is another common casting transgression, especially by frustrated casters who are not seeing forward line extension and crisp turnover with

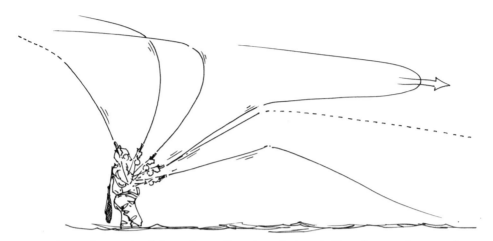

A complete overhead forward cast. Stop the rod about halfway between horizontal and vertical to complete loop formation and to transfer energy from the rod into the line in a forward direction. The rod does not drop to the horizontal fishing position until after the rod stop has occurred and the forward cast is straightening.

weighted rigs. When casters see their forward casts collapsing rather than extending over the water, the natural tendency is to muscle up, which usually results in the rod being powered even farther toward the water in a big, flailing arc. That pretty much kills loop control and forward energy transfer.

Transferring energy from the rod into the line is a lot like launching a taffy apple off a stick: The more hand speed you smoothly build and the more abruptly you stop the stick, the faster and farther the apple is going to fly. Acceleration alone without a sudden stop of the stick will not launch the apple on a fast, flat forward trajectory. Maximum energy transfer in a forward direction is dependent on that sudden stop occurring before the stick (or rod) reaches horizontal. If the stop comes too late, after the stick (or rod) has already reached or passed horizontal, then the apple (or fly line) is driven downward, not forward. For the greatest forward energy transfer, the stop should occur above horizontal and right after the wrist flip, which is the final and fastest period of acceleration.

Powering the rod too far toward the water also opens loops too dramatically for forward trajectory of a weighted payload (unless the line is very highly energized). Controlled loop formation is a critical aspect of casting all flies, including weighted nymphs. Tight, well-focused loops will drive fly lines and unweighted flies maximum distances. But moderately open loops, combined with sufficient line speed, are better suited for driving weighted rigs with few entanglements at all but extreme nymphing distances. Remember, with a weighted rig, you have a relatively heavy, bulky payload coming through on the forward cast. Loops that are moderately open allow that heavier strung-out rig more room to turn over cleanly without hitting the rod tip or fouling around the line or indicator. It's the same concept as roundhouse lobbing a wide open loop to prevent fouling a weighted rig, except that you're opening loops moderately by controlled degrees while maintaining sufficient line speed to achieve positive turnover of the weighted payload. As long as you maintain sufficient line speed, you will indeed get crisp turnover and excellent accuracy with surprisingly open loops out to about 50 feet, which covers the vast majority of nymphing situations.

Once your overhead casting technique is solid, controlled loop size is pretty simple to achieve. Loop size or shape is largely determined by the length and direction of the wrist flip. For a smaller or tighter loop on

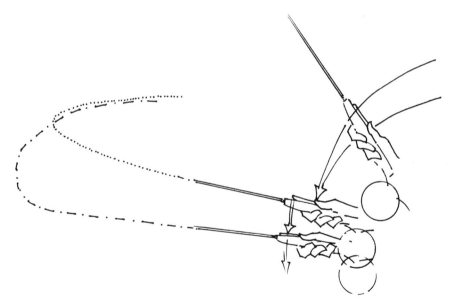

Loop size is largely determined by the length and direction of the wrist flip. To open your loops by controlled degrees, lengthen your wrist flip and arc your hand a bit as it moves down and forward through the flip. Remember, the path of the rod hand for most of the overhead forward cast should still be down and forward in a fairly straight line. Controlled arcing to intentionally open loops should be encapsulated within the wrist flip, which occurs late in the forward cast.

your overhead forward cast, shorten the wrist flip and keep your rod hand on a very straight path as it moves through the flip. For a more open loop on your overhead forward cast, lengthen the wrist flip and arc your rod hand more as it moves down and forward through the flip. To open your loops by controlled degrees, do not arc your rod hand excessively through the entire forward cast. Work on building controlled arc into just the wrist flip itself. The path of the rod hand for most of the overhead forward cast should still be down and forward in a straight line. Controlled arcing to intentionally open loops should be encapsulated within the wrist flip, which occurs late in the forward cast.

As you experiment with casting a weighted rig with the overhead forward cast, you will quickly see the direct correlation among loop size, the length of the wrist flip, and the amount of arc employed as the wrist flips forward and down. Play with opening your loops by controlled degrees until you reach a happy medium, with loops that are open enough to minimize fouling yet focused enough for clean forward trajectory and positive turnover at a given distance.

REARWARD DRIFT BEFORE THE FORWARD CAST

With the overhead forward cast, you will find that you can accelerate more smoothly to higher line speeds if you let your rod hand drift upward and back slightly after the backcast. Slight rearward drift of the rod hand also dampens the bouncing of a weighted rig at the end of an energized backcast. As you practice forward-casting weighted rigs, experiment with allowing a bit of rearward drift of your rod hand after the backcast to experience for yourself how it enhances control of the weighted payload on the backcast and sets you up for longer, smoother acceleration on the forward cast.

On a standard overhead backcast with the line unrolling upward and back, the rod hand should drift upward and back very calmly so it doesn't derail the direction or energy of the backcast. As the plane of the line on the overhead backcast changes to more horizontal, as it will as casting distance increases, the backward drift of the hand should become more horizontal to stay in the same plane as the backcast. As you begin to cast weighted rigs creatively with three-quarter, sidearm, and cross-body deliveries, keep the rearward drift of the rod hand very calm and in the same direction that your backcast is traveling.

THE STROKE-LENGTH AND TIMING DISPARITY

As you practice lifting a weighted rig off the water and delivering it right back after a single backcast, you should notice a stroke-length and timing disparity between your backcast and forward cast. The physical stroke length of an initial backcast is nearly twice as long as that of the forward cast. And on a three-count rhythm, an initial backcast and the pause to allow it to straighten consume almost two counts to the forward cast's one count. That's as it should be. Whenever you eliminate false casting, as you should strive to do in most of your nymphing, the backcast must perform two functions—the lift to aerialize the line and nymph, plus the backcast itself—whereas the forward cast has only the single function of making the forward delivery. That double function requires a longer stroke and more time. Work on developing an initial backcast stroke that is longer than your forward stroke and on allowing more time for the initial backcast, including the pause, than for the forward cast. You will use this casting stroke and rhythm regularly for pick-it-up, put-it-down nymphing, and it's a distinctly different stroke and rhythm than is used when false casting.

Some situations call for false-casting a weighted rig between pickup and delivery. Nymphing at extreme distances or shooting line to transition from a short to a long cast are typical false-casting scenarios. Once the line is already aerialized, as it is during false casting, the stroke length and timing between backcasts and forward casts are more even. Many anglers are so habituated to false casting and an even backcast–forward cast tempo that when they switch to pick-it-up, put-it-down nymphing, they tend to rush their forward casts, causing all kinds of control and delivery problems. Give an initial backcast a longer stroke and more time to straighten. Then make the forward cast.

For pick-it-up, put-it-down nymphing with weighted rigs, I use an asymmetrical three-count casting rhythm: "one-two" for the backcast and the pause, and "three" for the forward delivery. In my head, the tempo is "da-da, da." Lift and straighten the backcast (da-da). Hammer down and forward on the delivery (da).

HAULING WITH WEIGHTED RIGS

To achieve nearly the same degree of accuracy with weighted rigs as with dry flies, you must maintain sufficient line speed to turn over the line, leader, and weighted rig crisply. As casting distances or headwinds increase, hauling will increase your line speed and boost line, leader, and rig turnover. As you work on honing your nymphing deliveries at moderate distances with the overhead cast and a fixed line length, be aware that accuracy is closely tied to line speed and is highly dependent on crisp turnover of the terminal rig. If line speed drops off and the turnover stalls out at any point in the forward cast, accuracy stalls out along with it, which is why lobbing weighted rigs is no better for achieving accuracy than it is for distance.

Hauling—pulling on the line to shorten and accelerate the line during the backcast, the forward cast, or both (double hauling)—is much more than a long-distance casting technique. Hauling has broad application for casting at very ordinary ranges, especially with weighted nymphs.

Hauling helps energize the line for excellent extension on the initial backcast, which largely eliminates the need to false-cast, making your nymphing much more efficient. I routinely haul to help straighten my initial backcast with authority, even if it is a short one. Hauling and shooting line on the backcast (back shooting) zip line retrieved during the previous presentation back out through the guides, setting you up for a relatively long forward cast without false-casting.

As you nymph your way through a variety of water types with different presentations, you're going to be confronted with an array of challenging pickups. You may need to pick up a long line, pick up starting from a high rod position, or pick up and backcast into a stiff wind. In each case, hauling during the backcast helps aerialize the fly line and your submerged nymph before you've burned too much of your backcast stroke; that translates into longer, smoother acceleration and better control of weighted rigs. Your single biggest tool for getting nymphs airborne and avoiding the need to false-cast excessively in your nymphing is to haul on your initial backcast. Haul routinely on the short backcasts as well as the long ones.

Specifically, I often begin to haul on the backcast just before the weighted rig leaves the water. That's the point in the backcast at which acceleration can easily bog down and your timing can fall apart, especially if you're starting the pickup from a high rod position or the nymph is still a few feet deep. Beginning the haul when it's time for the weighted rig to exit the water keeps overall acceleration smooth. With a deep-drifting rig, my haul on the initial backcast is often more forceful than one on a forward cast. With experience, you'll learn to vary the intensity of the backcast haul as needed to get the rig airborne smoothly.

Accuracy with weighted rigs is closely tied to maintaining sufficient line speed for crisp turnover of the terminal rig. Hauling on the forward cast increases line speed substantially and is your single biggest tool for achieving crisp turnover of weighted rigs. It will improve your accuracy with weighted rigs at all ranges.

Hauling on the forward cast is often essential for turning weighted rigs into the teeth of a stiff wind. Without the extra line speed generated by hauling, weighted rigs are particularly prone to stalling out in the wind and drifting off target. But with that extra line speed, weighted rigs will turn over into stiff blows with enough oomph to stay on target.

Hauling is an essential skill for shooting line with all flies, weighted or unweighted. The ability to shoot weighted nymphs is a major asset on lakes and rivers, but it's also a very underappreciated advantage on small creeks. Small-stream trout are highly susceptible to predators, particularly herons, and are often the most skittish and unapproachable trout of all. Shooting weighted rigs accurately allows you to work nervous small-stream trout from a secretive distance. In my small-stream guiding, I find that anglers who can't haul and shoot weighted rigs are routinely out of business on the long, slow refuge slicks where inactive trout often pod up. And on windy days, anglers who don't haul effectively have trouble operating at ordinary ranges.

As you begin to haul regularly, casting weighted rigs becomes surprisingly effortless, even with light trout rods and substantial payloads. Since hauling can double the speed of the line, you need less rod-arm energy and less rod travel to cast a given distance, and that keeps the majority of your nymphing relaxed, efficient, and very controlled. When you need to really reach out, you can combine double hauling with longer, more vigorous rod strokes to shoot weighted rigs impressive distances. Keep your hauling with weighted rigs smooth and relaxed, even at long distances. An explosive haul on the final forward cast in an effort to generate extra distance can easily bounce a weighted rig or the rod tip and unhinge the entire delivery.

When I'm stretching my casting range with a weighted rig, I like to keep weight concentrated close to the nymph. If there is a slight flaw in timing or stroke, a strung-out rig with split shot widely separated from the nymph is much more likely to tumble and foul. My sight fishing on lakes often calls for 70-foot-plus casts and a nymph that sinks quickly to intercept fast-cruising trout; for that style of nymphing, I tie most of my nymphs with sufficient weight wrapped into their foundations. If I need to add shot to increase the sink rate of a nymph when I'm casting at extreme ranges, I usually slide the shot tight to the hook eye.

The quickest way to integrate hauling into your actual nymphing is to forget about double hauling at first and concentrate on single hauling to accelerate your backcasts. Once your backcasts are consistently controlled and energized, then it's quite simple to also haul on the forward cast, at which point you're double hauling.

As you begin to double haul weighted rigs, don't revert to excessive false casting. Remember, in nymphing, much of the point of double hauling is to eliminate or minimize false casting at all but extreme nymphing ranges.

HAMMERING

At typical nymphing distances of 20 to 40 feet, I can achieve excellent accuracy with a weighted rig and loops that are surprisingly open as long as I maintain sufficient line speed to turn over the rig with plenty of zip. Consequently, for casting substantial weight at short to moderate ranges, I often use relatively open loops, which are virtually tangle-free, with line speed as the major component of accuracy. On an overhead forward cast, I hammer down and forward with extra acceleration during the forward wrist flip before stopping the rod near horizontal. The resulting loop is quite open, but the short to moderate length of line is so completely energized that when the rod stops, the line, leader, and weighted rig really kick over anyway. The deviation from standard overhead casting is not great. At the end of the forward cast, the rod hand simply hammers down a bit harder and farther than usual. As you hammer down crisply through the wrist flip, your rod hand will arc or sweep a bit at the end of the forward stroke, and your loop will automatically open for tangle-free delivery as your nymph rig pops over with plenty of velocity and right on target.

As casting distance increases, you need progressively tighter loops and a higher rod stop on the forward cast to zing the payload on a forward trajectory. You can achieve excellent accuracy with relatively open and tangle-free loops out to surprising ranges, however, as long as you really energize the fly line. Once you have the hang of hammering at short to moderate ranges with open loops off the overhead cast, you will naturally begin to apply hammering to zip weighted rigs at longer ranges. You can hammer quite forcefully over shorter wrist flips to energize the line while progressively closing up loops by controlled degrees. And you can hammer more forward than down as the plane of the line shifts toward horizontal for longer casts.

For most of my nymphing, I combine hammering and hauling with the most open loops that will turn the weighted payload crisply at a given distance. That virtually eliminates fouling when casting at all but extreme ranges, where loops must be tightened up and timing and stroke must be very precise to prevent fouling.

Hammering is tailor-made for slinging weighted rigs at high speeds, because it delivers peak rod speed exactly when and where it's needed—at the end of the forward stroke after the weighted rig has already been smoothly accelerated. And, very importantly, hammering is encapsulated within the wrist flip, where loop shape is largely determined, making it highly adaptable to most casts and distances. As you begin to hammer really well on a variety of casts at a variety of ranges, it is a sweet sensation; you feel the rod smoothly loading and unloading right into the butt. And those weighted payloads go right where you intend with impressive zip and surprisingly little effort or fouling.

Hammering, because it imparts maximum rod acceleration at the correct and critical point in the forward cast, is very relaxing. It does not require violent force or exertion. On the contrary, the application of power is very controlled and efficient. Glide smoothly through the forward stroke on a clean, controlled path, not a flailing arc, and then hammer crisply through the wrist flip, as if you are driving a nail. Since the rig turns over very positively and accurately, you'll find yourself covering more water with fewer casts. Minimal false casting, a single accurate presentation to most stations, your weighted rig punching through the surface and dropping quickly to productive depths . . . prospecting with a nymph doesn't get much more efficient than that.

JABBING

Hauling and hammering are major techniques for generating plenty of line speed to turn weighted rigs crisply and accurately. Jabbing is a minor technique that is handy for delivering extra oomph late in the cast to prevent turnover from stalling out. I often jab when the wind is gusting in my face or I'm casting a weighted rig on a tippet that is too long or light to turn the rig easily.

Jabbing is simple: Complete the forward power stroke and drop the rod to horizontal; as the leader begins to turn over, jab the elbow of your rod arm back. This shortens the line a foot or more very late in the delivery to really goose leader turnover.

TUCK CAST

On a tuck cast, a weighted nymph rig kicks over and hits the water ahead of the fly line, punching through the surface and sinking quickly as slack leader piles in on top of the cast. That makes the tuck cast excellent for sinking a nymph quite vertically in current, along sharp drops, or with minimal weight—all of which makes tuck casting extremely useful for general nymphing.

Tuck-casting a weighted rig is simple. Just make a standard overhead cast and haul on the forward cast while stopping the rod tip high and abruptly. Hauling combined with a short but vigorous wrist flip provides the acceleration you need to really pop the rig over with a shortened forward stroke.

To tuck cast, make a standard overhead forward cast. Stop the rod tip high on the delivery and bounce it backward a bit. The weighted rig should turn over into an abrupt dive hitting the water ahead of the line. Slack line and leader piles in on top of the nymph, allowing for a fast vertical sink.

Immediately after stopping the rod high on the forward cast, bounce your rod hand back sharply just an inch or two. That bounce helps the weighted rig turn over into an abrupt dive.

In addition to using a tuck cast to sink a nymph quickly, I tuck for accuracy at very short ranges. With only a few feet of line beyond the rod tip, it's difficult to develop much line speed or accuracy with most casts, but a tuck cast combined with a haul will turn a weighted rig with good velocity and accuracy on a very short line.

The tuck cast is great for nymphing on creeks with overhanging grass. With a short line and a high rod stop, the trajectory of the nymph to the water is straight down, allowing the nymph to be tucked over the top of overhanging grass or brush and into small openings. Since the rod stops high when you tuck, you're in excellent position to manipulate short drifts or short, teasing swings and to strike instantly when lightning-quick trout dart from cover to grab the nymph on impact, which is very common as you learn to tuck precisely in close quarters.

Tuck casting delivers excellent accuracy in high winds, because the weighted rig is driven downward toward the water with enough velocity that it takes a powerful gust to move it off course. On windy days, I often tuck-cast to stay on target out to about 50 feet (since tucking drives the fly downward, it's not conducive to shooting the fly long distances, although you can shoot extra slack into the cast as the nymph dives toward the water). To tuck cast out to about 50 feet or over obstacles at close range, elevate your rod hand overhead for the entire backcast and forward cast; that gives you the room to use a longer stroke while still checking the rod tip high on the forward delivery.

TILTING THE ROD PLANE

Many situations call for tilting the rod plane from overhead to sidearm or some angle in between. Casting sidearm—tilting the rod plane 90 degrees from vertical to horizontal—lets you backcast or forward cast low to the water and under obstructions. Using a short fly rod and casting sidearm are standard operating procedure on small wooded streams. In very tight quarters, I often cast sidearm but pull my rod hand and forearm in tight to my chest and cast with very little hand travel. If your hauling and loading are precise, you can cast weighted rigs with decent velocity and accuracy at average nymphing ranges of 20 to 40 feet using less than a foot of rod-hand travel and almost no arm travel.

Casting sidearm allows you to keep an entire cast low to the water, where it's less exposed to wind. On streams with high banks, wind speed is often dramatically lower close to the water than it is 10 feet up. Even on wide open rivers, wind speed is usually lower and more manageable close to the water. Tilting the rod plane lower also keeps your rod and fly line less visible to fish, particularly on sunny days, when rod shafts and fly lines emit flash.

The ability to tilt the rod to any plane lets you guide your casts between obstructions. For example, by late summer, a narrow but usable casting lane often exists between high weeds and low tree limbs, but you have to be able to tilt the rod plane at will to use most of those lanes. For many anglers, casting with the rod plane slightly tilted, rather than vertical, is more natural and comfortable. For casting average distances without wind or obstructions, I usually tilt the rod plane about 20 degrees below vertical.

Tilting the rod plane lower makes it easier to reach well back on your backcast. This helps you make those long casting strokes to accelerate weighted rigs smoothly. When I'm double hauling for maximum distance with a weighted rig, I tilt the rod plane about 45 degrees (halfway between vertical and horizontal) and reach well back on the backcast. That gives me more room to accelerate in both directions.

Once you're casting weighted rigs crisply and accurately with the overhead cast, it's easy to tilt the rod plane all the way down to sidearm, or to any angle in between. To tilt the rod plane, get in position to make a standard overhead pickup, with the palm of your rod hand vertically oriented as if you are going to make a karate chop straight down. Now simply rotate the forearm of your casting arm outward *before* beginning the pickup; try this without the rod first. With a 90-degree outward rotation of the forearm (from the vertical karate-chop position), your palm faces straight up, and you are positioned to make a sidearm backcast and forward cast. With various rotations of less than 90 degrees, you're ready to cast on any rod plane between overhead and sidearm. After rotating the forearm the desired

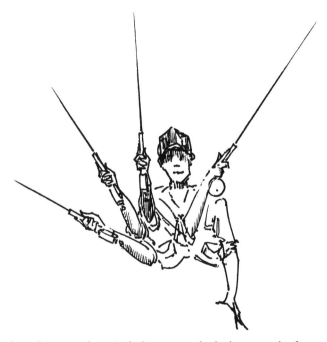

To tilt the rod in any plane, including across the body, rotate the forearm of your rod arm before *beginning the backcast. The illustration shows various planes within the backcast stop position. A great way to develop a feel for tilting the rod is to make karate chops in different planes. Rotate your forearm to put your hand in the desired chopping plane before making the backward stroke. Then maintain that same rotation throughout the back and forward chop.*

amount before beginning the pickup, maintain the same basic stroke and timing that you use for the overhead cast. You should see no dropoff in line control or accuracy while casting on different planes.

When your overhead cast is sound, it's quite easy to tilt the rod to cast across your body and over your opposite shoulder (for a right-handed caster, that's casting over the left shoulder). The ability to sling weighted rigs crisply and accurately with cross-body casts increases your available casting lanes and frequently improves your angle of presentation into a target.

If you're not already casting across your body, here's all it takes to get going: Make a standard overhead cast over your normal rod shoulder (if you're right-handed, your rod hand will stop near your right ear at the top of the backcast). Now make another overhead cast, but before starting the pickup, rotate your forearm slightly inward, about 20 degrees, so that the palm of your rod hand just begins to turn downward. On the backcast, tilt the rod slightly left of vertical and cross your rod hand in front of your body, stopping it by your left ear. That's all it takes to cast high over your off shoulder: Rotate your palm downward a bit before starting the pickup, then tilt the rod a bit past vertical and cross your rod hand in front of your body on the backcast. The stop position of the rod hand at the top of an overhead cross-body backcast simply shifts to the opposite side of your head—a lateral shift of barely 12 inches from a standard overhead cast. Other than that, it's the exact same backcast and forward cast. Practice those two casts alternately: a standard overhead cast over your rod shoulder, then a cross-body overhead cast. If your standard overhead cast is sound, making that slight shift in the backcast stop position to the opposite side of your head will feel natural in short order.

Once your overhead cross-body cast is sound, maintain the same stroke and tilt the rod plane progressively lower until you can work with the rod parallel to the water. To make a cross-body cast in a low rod plane, rotate your rod forearm inward a full 90 degrees, so that your palm faces down as you begin the pickup. Casting across your body in a full range of rod planes is a relatively easy transition with a substantial payoff. Suddenly you have the ability to cast while tilting the rod plane 180 degrees, from very low to the water off your right or left side, and every angle in between.

The ability to cast over your off shoulder doubles your pickup options. Say you are a right-handed caster but your normal backcast lane is blocked by a tree extending halfway over the stream from the right bank; just pick up over your left shoulder and backcast over the open left bank.

Once you can cast and pick up over your off shoulder, you'll begin to recognize plenty of opportunities to do both, and you'll find tight little streams much easier to contend with. You'll also find plenty of use for cross-body casting on big water. For instance, a stiff crosswind blowing from the right pushes the fly line into a right-handed caster; the solution is to cast over your off shoulder so that the line passes you safely on the downwind side. When fishing from a driftboat or canoe, you may need to work over your off shoulder to keep your loops safely away from other anglers in the craft.

ELLIPTICAL CASTS

In an elliptical cast, the backcast is made with the rod plane tilted toward sidearm, and the forward cast is made with the rod plane tilted more vertically toward overhead. To connect the two casts, as the backcast is straightening, calmly elevate your rod hand into position for a more overhead forward cast. Elevating the rod hand can be combined with some rearward drift to help maintain steady line tension and eliminate bouncing of a weighted rig at the end of an energized backcast.

An elliptical cast swings even a very heavily weighted rig outward and safely away from your body. Lobbing is essentially low-speed elliptical casting with an exaggerated roundhouse stroke. My standard cast with a weighted rig is slightly elliptical, with the rod plane tilted to about three-quarter arm on the backcast and a bit closer to overhead on the forward cast. But even with a big nymph and several BB shot, I routinely haul to generate significant line speed, and I rarely find outright lobbing with a big elliptical stroke to be necessary or advantageous.

Where backcast space is limited to a few yards, I often use an elliptical cast with a truncated backcast to use whatever space is available. To do this, make a low-energy backcast flip with the rod plane tilted to three-quarters or sidearm. The backcast will not be straightened. The flip is just to get some line mass traveling backward to help load the rod and energize the forward cast. As soon as you've made the flip and before the line can straighten behind you or hit obstructions, sweep your hand up and around and continue into a more vertical overhead forward cast. If you exaggerate that up-and-around sweep, you gain more space to smoothly accelerate the forward cast, and you maintain steady line tension though the backcast never straightens. This is a cast you'll soon learn to appreciate when backcast space is limited, which is frequently the case on wooded streams.

ROLL CASTING

The obvious advantage of the roll cast—the ability to make a forward cast without a backcast—makes it a universal skill for fishing in tight quarters.

Most anglers already know roll-casting basics, but there are a few points specific to roll-casting weighted rigs.

Getting a deep-drifting rig airborne can sap a lot of energy out of a roll cast. You can build greater and smoother acceleration by using a longer forward stroke, which you can set up by beginning the forward portion of the roll cast with your rod hand extended farther up and back than normal.

The longer you hesitate between the setup phase and the roll cast itself, the deeper a weighted rig sinks. Once you've drawn the rod back and the line is positioned for roll-casting forward, cut the cast loose without delay while the repositioned nymph is still near the surface.

In addition to the standard overhead roll cast, work on roll-casting with the rod tilted at low angles to cast under upper-level wind and low-hanging obstacles. Where backcast space is limited, overhead space is often at a premium too, so many roll casts must be made sidearm.

DOWNSTREAM LOADING

Downstream loading entails trailing the fly line and nymph rig downstream of your position, and then slinging the forward cast upstream directly off the water. With downstream loading, you can employ a full range of forward casts, including overhead casts, sidearm casts, cross-body casts, a long casting stroke to shoot line, a short stroke to tuck. If you practice slinging a variety of forward casts directly off the water, you'll find downstream loading applicable to a surprising number of casts and situations on all types of moving water from brushy streams to windswept rivers.

The key to accuracy and control on the forward cast is breaking water tension smoothly. Just as when backcasting a weighted rig off the water, to forward cast a weighted rig directly off the water, straighten the fly line and get the line tip moving toward you; then accelerate smoothly into the cast.

I use downstream loading regularly when nymphing upstream. After the upstream presentation, the line and rig are simply flipped downstream and allowed to fall to the water. In significant current, the line quickly straightens and you're set for the next upstream cast.

In addition to eliminating false casting, one of the beauties of downstream loading is that it, in effect, can be used to suspend your backcast indefinitely as you move to a new casting position or pause to study the water. If you've been nymphing at 40 feet and you want to move upstream a few yards before making another upstream cast of the same length, there's no need to spool a bunch of line or false-cast excessively to maintain line control. Simply flip the entire 40 feet of line and leader downstream and let

Downstream loading entails using the current to load the rod instead of an aerial backcast. The fly line and nymph rig are trailed downstream in the current, and the forward cast is made upstream directly off the water. Downstream loading while hugging one bank and forward casting sidearm is a great way to fish through brushy tunnels where overhead casting space is obstructed.

it trail in a controlled fashion as you wade. Likewise, if you see a good trout flash to your nymph but it doesn't take, flip the line downstream to maintain control indefinitely as you rest the fish and plan your next presentation.

When nymphing streams that tunnel through brush, I often hug one bank and use downstream loading to work my way upstream without aerial backcasts (as a right-hand caster, I usually hug the left bank so I can forward cast sidearm off my normal rod shoulder). That allows me to fish through brushy corridors that often prove to be trout sanctuaries simply because they are rarely fished effectively.

When the wind is really howling from behind, you can use downstream loading to avoid having to backcast into the wind (and you can aim your forward casts high for exceptional carry with the wind). I've used downstream loading to salvage some memorable days on wide open western rivers when 50-mile-an-hour gusts were hitting me from behind and traditional backcasts were not an option.

When the wind is howling downstream instead of upstream, fishing your way down can be the only sane and efficient option. In dirty water, I also primarily fish downstream. When nymphing downstream, you can still load the rod with water tension in lieu of a traditional backcast, but casting straight off the water with the line drifting toward you is trickier. In significant current, you may need to strip to maintain line tension prior to the forward cast. Hauling during the forward cast or lengthening the casting stroke will also absorb some slack created by the line drifting toward you.

Water tension can also be used instead of an aerial backcast on stillwater. When solo fishing from a canoe, I often let 40 or 50 feet of fly line trail behind me as I paddle; if I spot a cruiser, I can grab the rod and sling the cast straight off the water.

Using water tension to load the rod allows instant changes in casting direction, another valuable stillwater skill. Say you've just cast to your left when you glimpse a cruising trout to your right. Rather than picking up the line and false-casting several times as you turn your body to face right, simply cast across your body from left to right directly off the water.

Once you're slinging controlled casts directly off the water, it's quite easy to integrate a single haul and shoot line to increase your distance. Just keep the haul smooth and progressive to build steady acceleration without bouncing the rig.

THE ROLL-CAST PICKUP
The roll-cast pickup puts you in position to fully energize your initial backcast, which often eliminates the need for subsequent backcasts. After a conventional upstream dead-drift nymph presentation, as the nymph

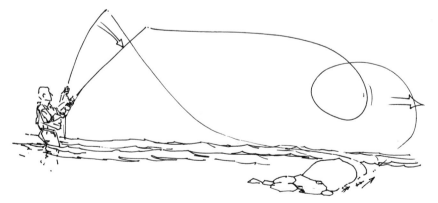

The roll-cast pickup is great for popping snagged nymphs off rocks from a discreet distance. Simply roll-cast a loop of line upward and beyond the snagged nymph to exert pressure from the far side and pop the nymph free.

approaches you, simply raise the rod tip and make a roll cast, but before the line falls to the water, transition into an energized backcast.

The roll-cast pickup is a good way to aerialize a deep-drifting nymph; the roll brings the nymph up and out of the water and gets some line mass moving forward. You could simply let the roll cast land and then fish it out, but transitioning into an energized backcast opens your options on the forward cast, allowing you to tuck, reach, or haul more effectively.

The roll-cast pickup is also great for freeing nymphs from rocky bottoms. Simply roll-cast a few feet of line beyond a snagged nymph to exert pressure from the far side. It will usually pop free.

THE HALFWAY CAST

Nymphing on lakes, and some of the most active and exciting nymphing on moving water, calls for long casts and retrieves. Whenever you strip in a lot of line and need to make another long cast with minimal false casting, the halfway cast is a practical solution.

The halfway cast entails learning nothing new; it's really more a strategy than a specific cast. After a lengthy retrieve, lay roughly half the line you intend to cast onto water you've already fished. Now you have significant line on the water, and it is well straightened for accelerating smoothly into a high-energy backcast. From there, double haul and shoot additional line. Often you can nymph 50 to 70 feet out with only two complete casting cycles, including the halfway cast, and with no aerial false casting, which can easily foul a weighted rig.

On lakes, using the halfway cast is the angling equivalent of staying locked and loaded; it keeps you primed for a fast delivery as you scan for cruising fish. As you're watching from a good vantage, lay enough line on the water to load the rod for a long cast with a single backcast; 40 feet of fly line on the water generally suffices. If the nymph starts to sink too deeply for easy pickup, make an occasional roll cast to reposition it near the surface. When you see a fast-moving cruiser, you're in position to immediately make a high-energy backcast and shoot additional line on the forward cast. Often you'll achieve all the distance you need without false-casting, and you'll get the nymph in front of a fish quickly before it disappears or cruises out of range.

CURVE CASTS AND AERIAL MENDS

In nymphing, some presentations call for very accurate casting, and others don't. But how your nymph behaves after it hits the water is a major factor in the success or failure of virtually every presentation. And controlling how the fly line lands on the water lets you control the behavior of your nymph from the moment of impact.

The tuck cast is essentially a vertical curve cast. In a well-executed tuck cast, the rod stops high and abruptly on the delivery, and the nymph dives or curves toward the water ahead of the fly line, with slack line and leader piling in on top of it for a very fast vertical sink. Because many situations call for a fast vertical sink, the tuck cast is easily the most useful cast in nymphing. If you practice tuck casting in various rod planes at short to moderate distances, it does not take long to establish excellent control of your tucks. And tucking, with its final burst of wrist acceleration and sudden rod stop, will teach you a ton about turning over weighted rigs on command.

A curve cast is essentially a tuck cast made horizontally so that the end of the fly line curves left or right instead of diving downward. Curves can be made to varying degrees in various rod planes, but for a right-handed caster, the most natural and pronounced curve is made by overpowering a sidearm cast to hook it inward (to the left). Accelerate the rod sharply before stopping it quite suddenly and sooner than normal, and bounce your hand backward a bit immediately after the rod stop. That bounce amplifies the curving of a weighted rig. Curves are great for hooking your nymph around obstacles. I often curve-cast to nymph the upstream face of a rock from a downstream position or to slide the nymph cross-current on an

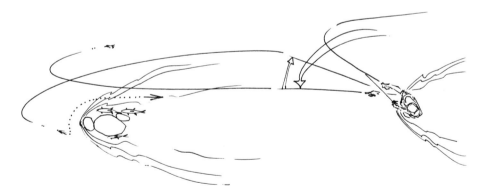

An inward curve cast is essentially a tuck cast made sidearm (rather than overhead) so that the fly line curves inward instead of diving downward. To exaggerate the inward curve of the line and a weighted nymph rig, stop a sidearm cast a bit sooner and sharper than usual, and bounce your rod hand backward immediately after the rod stop. Curves are great for stripping a nymph across current on an upstream presentation, including across the faces of upstream boulders.

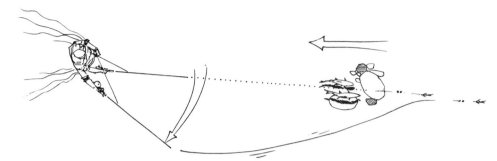

Right and left reach mends are great for countering drag and keeping the fly line off fish or prime water. To make a right reach mend, cast in any rod plane and simply reach to the right before the forward cast falls to the water. The reach repositions the fly line to fall outside the lane your nymph will drift through.

upstream presentation. An upstream curve cast helps sink a nymph very quickly if you land the curved end of the fly line and the leader upstream of the nymph.

The reach cast, more properly called a reach mend, since the reach is made after the casting stroke is completed but before the line falls to the water, is great for countering drag and keeping the fly line off fish or prime water. Right or left reach mends can be made while casting in any rod plane, but for starters, make a standard overhead cast, and as the line is straightening on delivery, simply reach the rod down and to the side. The reach repositions the fly line to fall outside the lane your nymph will drift through.

Unlike the tuck and curve casts, the reach mend is conducive to shooting flies considerable distances. When you need to cast a nymph right on target, remember that a reach mend angles the line into the target and will bring the nymph up short unless you shoot or cast some excess line to compensate.

The reach-back mend is simple to execute and puts you in precise control of your nymph on downstream presentations. I routinely use it when casting downstream to probe the upstream faces of boulders and logjams. Cast enough line to reach your target, but before the cast lands, reach back with the rod to check the cast several feet short of the target. As soon as the nymph hits the water, lower and extend the rod to feed slack and sink the nymph as it approaches the target. You can control the sink rate of the nymph by adjusting the speed of your feed. Giving complete slack allows the weighted nymph to plummet freely; feeding line downstream at a rate

The reach-back mend gives you precise control over the path, speed, and drop rate of downstream drifts. Cast enough line to reach your target, but before the cast lands, reach back and up with the rod to check the cast short. As soon as the nymph hits the water, lower the rod to feed slack and sink the nymph as it approaches the downstream target.

slower than the current creates resistance and hangs the nymph up in the current until you're ready to give slack and let it plummet. You can steer the nymph downstream precisely with the rod, and you can stop the downstream drift on a dime to hang or swing the nymph tight to hazards without snagging. Once the nymph is hanging downstream, reaching the rod right or left causes it to slide across current, which often pulls aggressive fish from under structure as they rush to nail escaping prey.

A downstream cast with a reach-back mend is tailor-made for dropping a nymph vertically where a riffle shelves suddenly into a deep cut. Trout love to sit on the bottom in the protected pockets just below riffles, but swift surface currents extending off riffles make it difficult to sink nymphs quickly into these pockets. A solution is to slowly feed a weighted nymph downstream through a riffle on a tight line, then give complete slack to let the nymph free-fall right off the edge of the shelf.

One of the beauties of the reach-back mend is that you can manually reposition the nymph with the rod before beginning the drift. If your downstream cast is not quite on target, just use the rod to steer the nymph into the desired current lane before feeding any line. That's an advantage you can use on blustery days, when wind is blowing casts off course, and for all kinds of tricky or exacting downstream drifts.

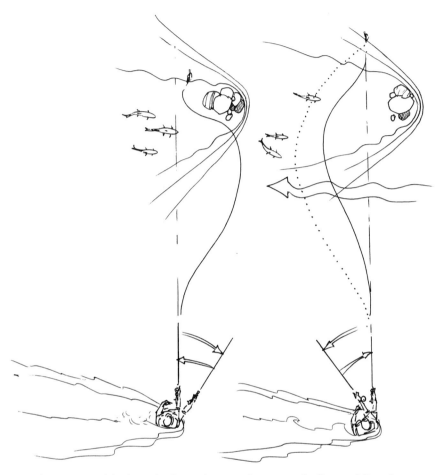

Reaching over and back as the forward cast settles causes the line to fall to the water in a curve. An upstream curve (left) *helps nullify drag. A downstream curve* (right) *bows the line to set up a controlled cross-current strip that slides the nymph over the snouts of trout facing into the current.*

If you can execute a right or left reach mend, you can execute a curve mend simply by reaching the rod to the side and back while the line is still in the air. Reaching over and then back causes the line to fall to the water in a curve. A sweeping over-and-back reach gives you a sweeping curve of the entire fly line. A quick over-and-back reach gives you a sharp curve over a short section of line. By adjusting the timing of the over-and-back reach, you control where on the fly line the curve occurs. You can curve around a specific obstacle or to nullify drag on a specific current lane. With a little practice, you can quickly progress from simple reach mends to more sophisticated curve mends.

Reach and curve mends are great for nullifying drag, but they can also let you create controlled drag. They are essential for intentionally bowing the fly line downstream to set up controlled cross-current swings, allowing you to regulate the depth, speed, and path of your swings as you probe pockets, cuts, boulders, and snags.

THE DETONATION FACTOR

The problem with high-speed, high-impact deliveries of weighted rigs is that they invariably spook trout, right? Whoa. Remember the last time a big brown trout charged 10 feet to nail your hopper imitation deposited on the surface with an audible splat? Well, on many days, trout charge, not flee, the splat of a weighted nymph—just as they charge the splat of a clumsy hopper, a caterpillar blown from a willow, or a frog jumping off a bank, or the disturbance of foraging baitfish.

Water is an excellent conductor of sound, and trout have a keen sense of hearing, although not of human voices or most sounds originating above the surface. Trout also detect very low-frequency vibrations, such as those emitted by swimming or wounded prey, through their lateral lines. Not surprisingly, trout rely heavily on their hearing not simply to detect danger, but also to locate prey. In nymphing, you can routinely use that to your advantage. When prospecting for scattered trout, I often plunk the nymph to grab the attention of trout and generate strikes. That's right, I intentionally put the nymph down hard.

In low light or murky water, typical prospecting situations, trout rely more heavily on their hearing to detect prey. In these situations, I routinely splat the nymph on the surface to create more audible attraction. I especially like to splat along undercut banks; trout that tuck under banks are confirmed ambushers and often react aggressively.

I detonate routinely on calm lakes and stream flats. Why? Because trout in quiet environments rely heavily on their sense of hearing to detect prey and to beat other trout to the chow. Additionally, trout that inhabit lakes and slow-stream flats are accustomed to moving for their food and will often charge an audible splat from several yards distant. There's not a more electrifying strike in fly fishing than a good trout charging and nailing a nymph on impact. The surface just churns, and you'd better have transferred the line to your pinch finger while the cast was still in the air.

During many nymphing sessions, especially if trout are highly aggressive and primed to strike opportunistically, I splat the nymph down on almost every cast. The splat can even trigger inactive fish, kick-starting them out of their lethargy. Watch the reaction of the trout. If the impact of the nymph attracts fish and triggers reflexive strikes, then splat away. If the splat of the nymph sends them bolting for cover, then back off and deliver more softly.

Typically it's not the impact of the nymph that scares trout—it's the impact of the fly line. Several forms of natural prey plunk down with an audible splat, but nothing edible to trout is 40 feet long and rips across the surface. If you keep the line off fish and off productive water that you haven't already probed, you'll be surprised how few trout are spooked by high-impact deliveries of weighted nymphs.

If I can see a trout on a shallow lie, I don't drop a weighted nymph directly on top of it. The instinctive reaction of most trout when bopped directly is to bolt, although I've seen many such trout bolt for just a few feet and then turn right around and nail the nymph. But if I can see a fish, I splat the nymph a few feet to one side and often a bit behind it. That eliminates any possibility of lining the fish, and a splat originating from a few feet away is much more likely to be greeted with curiosity than fright.

CHAPTER 3

Reasons to Move the Nymph

The purpose of this chapter is not to denigrate conventional dead-drift nymphing or dispute its effectiveness. On the contrary, dead-drift nymphing—drifting a nymph drag-free on a slack line at the same rate as the current—is an essential skill. When conditions warrant it, I mostly dead drift. Even when I'm primarily moving the nymph, I mix in conventional dead drifts when I see prime opportunities. And even during an active presentation, I usually dead drift at some point, particularly when I want to sink the nymph quickly.

The choice between dead drifting or moving the nymph is seldom an all-or-nothing proposition. Indeed, most nymphing calls for mixing and matching active and dead-drift tactics as you work through a variety of water types. The point of learning to move the nymph skillfully is not to abandon dead drifting, but to become an adaptable and versatile nymph fisher who can successfully deal with a gamut of presentation angles, depths, current speeds, and water conditions, and with the varying moods of the trout.

But specifically, how do you make the call whether to dead drift or move the nymph? There are a host of specific and legitimate reasons to move the nymph. But in general, dead-drift nymphing tends to imitate small and relatively common food forms in the drift, many of which are feeble swimmers. Conversely, actively stripping, pumping, or swinging the nymph tends toward what I call attractor nymphing, where a lively nymph, usually a substantial one, performs more as an attention-grabbing lure than a subtle and exacting food-form imitation. Attractor nymphing uses movement, along with sound, bulk, silhouette, color, and flash, to varying degrees to attract attention and elicit trout to strike out of predatory and territorial aggression, competitiveness, reflex, and hunger.

Above all, attractor nymphing is founded firmly on the principle that before a trout will eat a nymph for any reason, it must first detect the nymph. And in attractor nymphing, moving the nymph is your single biggest tool for both grabbing the attention of trout and triggering strikes.

AGITATING INACTIVE TROUT

May is prime time on my home waters, the fertile spring creeks that course the scenic valleys of southwestern Wisconsin's Driftless Area. An experience I had on a Wisconsin spring creek one May evening illustrates the value of moving the nymph to agitate inactive trout. But first an aside to put the trout fishing of the Driftless Area into a larger context for anglers who haven't fished there, and to make some important big-picture observations on selecting productive strategies for prospecting the water between hatches.

The Driftless Area is a rolling limestone upland spared by the last great glaciers that flattened most of the surrounding Midwest. The unglaciated hills extend across the Mississippi River into northeastern Iowa and southeastern Minnesota, which also have some excellent limestone streams, but Wisconsin is blessed with the lion's share of the Driftless Area, including more than a thousand miles of cold, clean spring creeks scattered over roughly a dozen counties. Some counties, including Vernon and Richland, have impressive concentrations of spring creeks, even compared with famed destinations such as Pennsylvania and Montana. A glance at the stream maps on pages 18 and 22 of the *Wisconsin Trout Fishing Regulations and Guide* can be a real eye-opener for anglers who are unaware of the sheer number of productive spring creeks in the region.

I began trout-fishing the Driftless Area with my father and grandfather almost as soon I could waddle along a creek bank. One of my earliest memories is of a glorious May morning sitting beside my paternal grandfather, Elmer, on the banks of Harker's Creek and catching my first ten-fish limit of German brown trout on crawlers and a cane pole. More than forty years later, I recall his comical consternation as I hoisted trout after trout and my fishing line into the barbed-wire fence behind us. My earliest nightmares revolved around a single recurring theme: that Elmer and my father would sneak out of the house before daylight to go trout-fishing without me. By kindergarten, I was wandering off on my own to fish with my Shakespeare Wonder Rod fly rod tipped with a freshly cut chub tail, which turned out to be an excellent foundation for later nymphing. As I sat in the first grade at Odana Elementary on Monday mornings following weekends of chasing trout, I'd fish Smokey Hollow again in my mind. Smokey was my favorite stream, and I had better than 2 miles of runs, riffles, holes, and cutbanks committed to memory in vivid detail—a budding facility for almost total recall of outdoor places and experiences that I never did extend to academic matters. As I gazed at the blackboard, I saw the image burned into my brain from weekends of dawn-to-dusk fishing—fly line on water.

In my lifetime, I've watched the angling population on my home waters transition from local catch-and-kill bait fishers to mostly catch-and-release fly casters from throughout the Midwest. Chicago and the Twin Cities are within a two- to four-hour drive of most of the Driftless Area, and I've spotted license plates from as many as half a dozen states in a day. The big draws are thriving populations of wild trout, dozens of decent to excellent streams to explore, and abundant access. Native brook trout are rebounding in many small headwater tributaries and a few main stems. Most streams support fair to exceptional densities of naturally reproducing brown trout. Browns thrive in the upper and middle reaches of many watersheds, but they also use marginal downstream habitat much more successfully than brook trout, so the bulk of the stream mileage is brown-trout water. Some of the biggest wild browns in the area, including the rare fish of 5 pounds or better, spawn in autumn in clean, gravelly headwaters. After spawning, they may drop downstream to large, more degraded lower watersheds, where they spend much of the year dining in solitude on abundant min- nows, shiners, and chubs, until summer heat or the fall spawning urge pushes them back upstream. Many watersheds have good to exceptional trout densities in their clean, cold headwaters and middle sections, and much lower trout densities in their larger downstream sections, but at the point in a given watershed where trout density begins to drop sharply, average trout size usually jumps. Spring is prime time for targeting trophy browns in the 20-inch class, particularly in lower watersheds. Trout metab- olisms are in high gear, and fish are often aggressive right through the mid- day hours, which allows you to prospect long stretches of stream very quickly with active nymph or streamer tactics as you hunt for scattered tro- phy fish.

Numerous Driftless Area streams have slot size limits that are designed to protect the majority of spawning-age fish. Stocking of hatchery strains is on the decline and is limited to a few put-and-take waters that have little or no natural reproduction. The emphasis is on stabilizing and improving habitat for wild trout, rather than put-and-take stocking of domestic trout. Where habitat has been improved, the state sometimes stocks wild-strain brown or brook trout to jump-start a wild, self-sustaining population. A rel- ative handful of Driftless Area waters are managed as catch-and-release fishing with only flies or artificial lures allowed. A few large, well-publicized special-regulation streams attract steady streams of fly fishers, including the bulk of nonresident anglers. Discovering waters that offer fine fishing and solitude requires a willingness to walk and devote significant fishing time to exploring out-of-the-way streams. I routinely walk more than 5 miles a day in fishing and scouting the area.

Overall, action for wild browns to 16 inches is superb, even when measured against the premier Rocky Mountain waters. (Having fished the West for a month or two a summer for much of the last thirty years, I'm in a fair position to compare.) Catching a couple dozen adult browns ranging from 12 to 16 inches is a solid day but is very achievable on good streams when fish are active. A few times each season, I nymph more than a dozen adult trout from a single run, and on occasion it's way over a dozen. Browns of 17 inches and larger make up less than 5 percent of the population in most streams but are common enough to be targeted with special nymph and streamer strategies. Browns to 16 inches rise freely to a variety of hatches, but the relatively small size of most creeks, coupled with our true four-season climate and rapid transitions between seasons, compresses most hatches into relatively short windows. Trout of a couple pounds or more simply can't count on feeding efficiently on the surface with regularity over extended periods of weeks or months, so they adapt. By the time Driftless Area browns attain about 17 inches and 2 pounds, they tend to specialize in feeding subsurface on sizable prey, including crayfish, minnows, small rough fish, and smaller trout. I often prospect with robust soft-hackle nymphs or Soft-Hackle Mini-Buggers in size 12, because they're a big enough mouthful to consistently move trout of all sizes, including top-end fish, yet small enough to be delivered precisely out to significant ranges on light trout rods. When I prospect Driftless Area streams with size 16 and smaller nymphs or with dry flies, my encounters with top-end fish drop dramatically.

Actually, it's pretty rare to see a Driftless Area brown of 17 inches or better sipping on the surface, even during a significant mayfly or caddis hatch. Whenever sizable trout are present in a population but rarely seen working the surface during hatches, that's a definite indication that you need to go subsurface with the bulk of your prospecting, and probably present a fairly substantial fly, if you're going to hook those fish with any consistency. That's the scenario that keeps me prospecting subsurface much of the time in the Driftless Area and developing a versatile array of nymphing skills, flies, and strategies. And it's a scenario that exists on the majority of local and regional fisheries where trout that are measured in pounds, rather than inches, constitute only a small percentage of the population.

That's in sharp contrast to my experience on many of the premier spring creeks and tailwater rivers of the Rockies where trout of 2 pounds or better abound and rise freely to abundant hatches. Where sizable trout can feed regularly and efficiently on the surface, they do. Since these trout are acclimated to looking up, they remain fairly receptive to rising to dry flies between hatches. On many Rocky Mountain fisheries, quite a few dry-fly prospecting strategies will put 2-pound and bigger trout on the end of a tippet with some regularity. In fisheries where 2- and 3-pound trout are abundant and frequently feed on the surface, top-end trout of 5 pounds or larger often specialize in feeding subsurface on relatively large food forms. Whatever the size of the top-end trout in a given fishery, solid subsurface skills will help you target them. When I reflect on my fishing throughout the Rockies, in almost every case the single biggest trout I've hooked on a given fishery hit while I was prospecting subsurface. That's true of the Madison, Upper Missouri, Ruby, Yellowstone, Paradise Valley spring creeks, Big Spring Creek at Lewiston, Snake, Green, Gunnison, Platte, Frying Pan, San Juan, the various forks and tributaries of the Flathead and Salmon, hundreds of high-country lakes, and scores of back-country streams. And that's true despite the fact that in the West, I spend considerable time matching hatches and prospecting with dry flies simply for the enjoyment of catching nice trout on top.

Most remarkable of all, public access to Wisconsin trout streams remains outstanding. That's particularly notable given the rush toward privatization of trout water across much of the country. Wisconsin has extremely liberal stream access laws. The state owns the streambeds, and anglers can legally wade any navigable stream as long as they don't step out of the stream onto private lands without permission, though it is legal to leave the stream temporarily to skirt obstacles, including fence crossings and driveways. Virtually all streams large enough to support trout are considered navigable. Since anglers can legally wade-fish nearly all streams anyway, private landowners generally allow angling access across their property. If a particular landowner denies access, anglers can still wade and fish through that property as long as they get into the water legally from a public bridge right-of-way, a public easement, or neighboring land where they have permission. Where state trout stamp funds are used to improve habitat, the state secures long-term fishing easements, so there are also hundreds of public fishing easements where anglers can legally walk streambanks. All in all, there are very few stream sections that can't be legally fished. Liberal access gives the angling public a large stake in the well-being of these spring creeks, resulting in more active angling organizations and increased funds and manpower for improving and protecting streams.

Before settlement, native brook trout were abundant, with fish commonly running to a few pounds. By the 1930s, Driftless Area spring creeks as a whole were badly eroded and silted by unsustainable grazing and plowing practices in the surrounding hills. With little vegetation to retard runoff into the narrow valleys, streambeds were ravaged repeatedly by spring floods and major thunderstorms. Stream photos from the era are stark testimonials to the raw power of unchecked erosion; the larger streams had silted channels and collapsing dirt banks, sometimes in excess of 20 feet high. Specific streams continue to be damaged or threatened, but land use has changed significantly in recent decades, and many watersheds have rebounded to become excellent wild trout habitat once again.

The biggest visual change from early settlement times has been to the hills, which were open prairie dotted with scattered oak groves when the first plows arrived. Into the first decades of the twentieth century, farmers burned the hills regularly to keep brush at bay, much as natural fire cleared the prairie for millennia. When regular burning ceased, much of the land, especially the steep hillsides, which are poorly suited to crops or grazing, transitioned to brush and hardwoods. Today maturing hardwood forests cloak hills that teem with white-tailed deer and wild turkeys, but in my teens I knew a few old-timers who remembered the Driftless Area as wide open oak savanna.

As family dairy farms of a few hundred acres have shut down in droves, considerable farmland has been sold for country home sites and recreational purposes. One benefit to trout has been increased absorption of precipitation because of decreased compaction of soil by cattle. Spring flows are improving, and some springheads that have been dry for decades are reemerging. Springs flow from limestone and sandstone formations year-round at just under 50 degrees Fahrenheit, and increased spring flows cool more stream mileage in summer, extending year-round trout habitat into the larger downstream portions of some watersheds. Increased spring flows and nutrient loads benefit the entire food chain, including aquatic insect and scud populations.

A Civilian Conservation Corps (CCC) camp established at Coon Valley in Vernon County during the Great Depression provided desperately needed employment for many, one Elmer Osthoff among them. The CCC conducted a landmark erosion control project in the Coon Creek watershed, which now supports some of the highest trout densities in the Drift-less Area. After leaving Coon Valley, my grandfather went on to a career surveying contour strips and flood-control dams for the Iowa County Soil Conservation Service. His job kept him in contact with farmers and local trout streams. Once, over lunch break, he located a pair of monster brown trout in a small creek south of Dodgeville. The one he caught wound up tipping a meat scale at nearly 8 pounds.

Today fishing organizations, most notably Trout Unlimited and the Fed-eration of Fly Fishers, assist the state with funding and manpower to stabi-lize streambanks against flooding and improve in-stream habitat for trout. Additional federal funding for habitat restoration is generated primarily by excise taxes on fishing equipment. The LUNKER structure, which stands for Little Underwater Neighborhood Keepers Encompassing Rheotactic Salmonids (how's that for stretching the English language to create a catchy acronym?), is a Wisconsin innovation. And the Driftless Area is LUNKER central, with several thousand LUNKERs in these spring creeks. LUNK-ERs are three-sided, open-framed, wooden fish cribs that are installed directly into streambanks and anchored with rods, limestone slabs, and earth to create artificial cutbanks. They are designed to withstand substantial floods, and along with rock riprap, they help stabilize banks while providing critical overhead escape cover for small-stream trout from their major pred-ators, herons and humans topping that list. Individual LUNKERs measure about 8 feet long, 3 feet wide, and a foot high. On sizable runs, two or more are often linked to form a long cutbank.

An entire pod of inactive trout can tuck inside a LUNKER that's installed in a foot or two of water, or trout can retreat completely under one that's installed just under the waterline in several feet of water. Nymphing these structures is a skill unto itself, with the perfect drift varying from run to run and influenced by current combinations and streambed configura-tions that are as individual as fingerprints. Consistently putting nymphs into or under structures without constantly putting the hook into wood requires precise casting and line control, as well as considerable experience in read-ing and fishing LUNKERs. On any given run, I usually prospect the most open feeding stations to pick off the most active and vulnerable trout before making risky presentations tight to a structure. If I do hang up in a struc-ture, I often wade close and pick the nymph off with my rod tip. If wading flushes a big brown, then I have that fish marked for subsequent visits.

Preventing a top-end brown of 3 pounds or better from breaking off in a structure is usually a seesaw affair. A big brown in a small stream invari-ably has a nose for protective cover (natural or man-made) and often has to surge only a foot or two to bury itself. The best position to fight from is usually on the opposite side of the stream and straight across from the structure; if you hook a big brown while standing on top of a LUNKER, the fish can bury back under your feet. After hooking a big trout, you may need to hustle upstream or down or charge across the channel to get opposite the structure and gain enough leverage to pressure the fish toward the middle of the stream. Once you get a big brown out from a structure, keep it out at all costs—it's better to risk breaking the leader or pulling the hook out than to let the fish into structure. A strong trout will bore repeatedly to reach cover, but if you can blunt the first hot charge or two, you have a good chance of steering the fight into open water. When you have to keep a big, strong trout on a very short leash, use the entire rod to absorb shock and cushion the tippet. At points in the fight when the tippet is really being taxed, I point the butt cap of the rod right at the fish to put the rod into a deep bow. That temporarily reduces rod-butt leverage and my ability to steer the trout, but it maximizes the shock absorbency of the entire rod shaft, which can be critical when you have to stop a strong fish in its tracks without giving an inch of line. As soon as a crisis point in a battle passes, I return to pressuring and steering the fish with a straighter rod using more butt leverage.

Most LUNKER structures are installed on outside bends or curves, where flood currents are greatest. Many straight runs are reconfigured without the use of LUNKERs. Often the riffle at the head of a run is channeled through a narrow rock chute, and a deep run is scooped below the chute. The swift entry chute oxygenates the water and helps scour the deep scoop clean of sediment. Big limestone slabs weighing hundreds of pounds are often plunked into these runs to provide trout with shade and physical cover. Where a narrow chute enters a broader run, there is a back eddy on each side of the entry chute. Fast chutes, abrupt depth changes, big boulders to impede clean drifts, conflicting current speeds and directions—nymphing these runs successfully calls for more than standard dead-drift tactics.

One of the beauties of small streams is that they respond dramatically to a little tender loving care. A single willing landowner and a half-mile habitat project can dramatically improve wild fish populations on a given branch, and a number of such projects can revitalize the trout population in an entire watershed. Where habitat is improved, wild trout populations typically increase several hundred percent within a few years. Many Driftless Area streams now have several hundred trout per mile, and some large high-quality streams have more than a thousand trout per mile.

Habitat improvement benefits trout in many ways. Stable banks result in narrower channels, faster current, cleaner spawning gravel, and improved bottom habitat for many prey organisms. Narrow streams also run cooler than wide, shallow streams. The increase in secure refuge cover provided by LUNKER structures and deep, boulder-studded runs is a tremendous boon to small-stream trout populations. With secure refuge cover and a catch-and-release ethic, streams that are narrow enough to be broad-jumped in places can support excellent numbers of adult trout, even in the face of considerable angling pressure.

One drawback of habitat projects is that they usually attract more anglers to a stream. If I'm already enjoying fine fishing with little competition on a piece of natural water, I almost hate to see that water improved. But as more and more Driftless Area streams are rehabilitated, angling pressure tends to become better distributed. I'm fishing a lot of rehabilitated water in the Driftless Area where I'm seeing surprisingly few anglers, even on weekends. As the total mileage of wild trout water increases, any angler with an exploratory bent should be able to find good fishing and elbow room.

It's amazing what you will occasionally stumble upon if you explore habitually. One of my current ace-in-the hole streams is not even generally known to be productive trout water. A decade ago, it was tepid chub water, but improved land-use practices in the surrounding watershed have cooled and cleaned the stream enough that wild browns have become established. They are chowing down on the abundant baitfish and are exhibiting exceptional growth rates. On one recent visit, I landed more than a dozen thick-bodied browns ranging from 17 to 19 inches, plus a couple dozen smaller but very stocky browns to 15 inches. That would be a pretty respectable day on wild brown trout on any big-name river in the Lower 48.

As for those crowded special-regulation streams, there are strategies for enjoying them when the fish are turned on and nobody else is around. I love to run and gun the popular spring creeks with a big, dark nymph and active nymphing tactics as chocolate water is just beginning to clear after a major storm. Typically the fish have been hunkered down for a day or two and are ready to feed, and competition from other anglers is nil. Last season, on a dirty-water Saturday in May, I jumped into the West Fork of the Kickapoo at Avalanche—the busiest month on the busiest stretch of the busiest catch-and-release trout stream in the entire Driftless Area—and blew through more than 3 miles of water in just a few hours as I nymphed several dozen brown trout and brookies, without bumping into another angler.

If you're ambitious enough to outhustle the crowds and strategic enough to turn angling access and use patterns to your advantage, there are many strategies for enjoying exceptional fishing in solitude. On a world-class public fishery, like New Mexico's San Juan River, that may mean donning your waders at 4 A.M. in some sprawling parking lot that will not begin to fill with glistening SUVs for several more hours. On the Green River below Flaming Gorge, it may mean positioning yourself 3 miles from the closest access point in late evening while everyone else is clumped within half a mile of the access point and ready to make a quick getaway when the bats come out and the canyon goes pitch black. Sometimes it's fishing in the morning where the squadrons of driftboats won't arrive until afternoon, fishing in the afternoon where the driftboat traffic clears in the morning, or wade fishing where driftboat fishing isn't allowed or isn't practical. Sometimes it's slipping and sliding into a canyon, walking over a big river bluff, or walking or wading distances that most anglers won't contend with. Sometimes it's targeting specific segments of the trout population, such as eddy cruisers, or specific water types that most anglers are ignoring. Locally, I enjoy some of my best fishing on lightly fished streams that have only scattered pockets of good habitat. On these "marginal" streams, I routinely walk several miles round-trip from my vehicle to cherry-pick a few productive runs. If I cherry-pick two or three marginal streams in a day, that can easily add up to fishing a dozen or more substantial runs that few other anglers even know of, providing a very worthwhile day of fishing.

At the point in many Driftless Area watersheds where trout densities begin to drop sharply as a result of habitat degradation or marginal water temperatures, fish size often jumps dramatically, because scattered trout are gorging on abundant baitfish. This phenomenon occurs on watersheds all over the country, and the perfect time to hit these low-density downstream waters is when trout metabolisms are in high gear and the fish are primed to blast a streamer or substantial nymph on the first presentation. That allows you to quickly prospect with an active fly through high volumes of water as you target widely scattered fish. On a recent April afternoon, I fished some 4 miles of a marginal Wisconsin stream and caught exactly two trout for my efforts, but they were beefy browns of 18 and 21 inches—exactly the kind of trout my presentations and strategy were geared to.

Presentation—the placement and behavior of your nymph—is always important, but nymphing at its most productive means fishing the right presentation with the right strategy. Presentation and strategy should be inextricably linked every time you string a rod. It's never just how you fish a given nymph. It's also when and where you fish it.

The open season on Driftless Area streams runs from early March through September. In March and April, fishing is restricted to artificial lures and catch-and-release on all streams. April is my busiest guiding month, with fly fishers enjoying some excellent early-season prospecting and hatch matching ahead of the general season. Opening weekend of the general season in early May touches off a flurry of catch-and-kill bait and spin fishing that quickly subsides. As summer arrives, with its heat, humidity, biting bugs, and high weeds, fly-fishing pressure also dwindles, and many of the remaining anglers make the mistake of concentrating on user-friendly pasture streams that are relatively large and warm and don't fish particularly well in hot weather. In sweltering summer heat, I enjoy excellent nymphing and some explosive terrestrial fishing in complete solitude by bushwhacking in to small, overgrown headwater streams, where water temperatures rarely top 62 degrees F even when air temperatures surge into the 90s. Not that Wisconsin simmers all summer; we're far enough north that we catch some gorgeous summer weekends with low humidity and days in the 70s.

Whatever the conditions in August, with the longer, cooler nights of September, water temperatures revert toward spring patterns, and midday fishing improves throughout the area as trout metabolisms are reinvigorated. By September, some large adult browns from degraded lower watersheds are moving upstream in search of suitable spawning sites; some years, spawning activity begins in late September while fishing season is still open. Big, aggressive browns can suddenly show up in small headwaters, and they respond well to attractor nymphing tactics and hot colors. I often fish a black Soft-Hackle Woolly Worm with a lively hot orange tail, a long tuft of underfur and guard hairs taken from a Zonker strip or hare hide.

I often fish several neighboring streams in a day. Over the seven-month season, I catch trout in as many as fifty different streams. I like to check out as many streams as possible early in the season so I can return to the hot ones as the season progresses. Having dozens of productive spring creeks within a couple hours of home keeps me fishing trout regularly, learning new strategies, and developing new skills, even in the years when the highest and most westerly peaks I see are the Mississippi River bluffs. I still crave traveling expansive country and fishing storied waters, especially in the West, where nearly every mountain range and river valley resounds for me with hitchhiking, backpacking, and fishing experiences. And it always gives me a big kick to see nymphing skills and strategies honed on local creeks transfer well to big-name rivers, especially when the fishing is not as easy as advertised and angling egos up and down a river are taking a visible pounding. But more than ever, I appreciate having good trout water near home, just for the opportunity to slip into it frequently.

On balance, May is the most vibrant and productive month to fish the spring creeks. The leaves on the hardwoods are newly erupted. The pastures are lush with green grass shot through with dandelions. Streamside weeds that will soon be head-high are just reaching the knee. Significant caddis, mayfly, or cranefly hatches are occurring frequently. Soft spring showers often color the streams nicely, making trout easier to approach. And invigorating water temperatures can make for productive prospecting right through midday.

Which brings me back to that May evening in the Driftless Area that I mentioned at the beginning of this chapter. On this particular Sunday, I was wrapping up a three-day weekend of solo fishing and camping and wanted to savor another hour of a beautiful May evening before heading home. The stream I was on holds a population of browns that is rather spotty except for a few scattered runs that are loaded with fish. I knew of a legitimate honey hole a quarter-mile walk upstream, and with time running short, I made a beeline for it. The run was pretty much as I remembered it. The headwater riffle deflected off the base of a steep hill, and the stream veered sharply into a wide open horse pasture, with strips of high willow whips lining both banks. During bouts of high water, current deflecting off the hill scoured the run clean so that it carried good depth of 3 to 5 feet along the far bank and down the center trough for about 15 yards. Relative to the surrounding stretches of shallow water, it was a major run with plenty of feeding stations and secure refuge water to harbor a few dozen trout.

When I arrived, only a few small trout were rising sporadically. I knew for a fact that more and bigger trout were present, so I slipped through the willows, eased into the lower end of the run, and began nymphing upstream. To avoid pushing a shock wave through the smooth run, I kept my feet anchored, and I prospected upstream by lengthening each successive cast by a few feet. My rod was already rigged with my bread-and-butter prospecting nymph for the region, a size 12 Soft-Hackle Woolly Worm in black and grizzly, plus a couple medium split shot. Soon I was dropping the weighted rig at the base of the riffle some 50 feet upstream and achieving nice, long dead drifts just off bottom. But more than a dozen enticing drifts right down the gut of the run produced nary a bump. Whatever these fish had spent their day doing, I'd arrived during a lull in their feeding rhythms. I'd worked an excellent caddis hatch several miles downstream for much of the day, and perhaps these fish had also gorged on emerging caddis. I couldn't see through the evening glare to observe bottom details, but I knew that inactive fish would be bunched down there in quiet depressions where they could hold with little effort. Since I was already fishing a proven prospecting pattern, rather than change flies, I changed tactics. I added enough shot to the tippet to put the nymph quickly near the bottom and pumped and teased it downstream through the deepest parts of the trough, bouncing it occasionally off the firm bottom. *Wham.* On the first presentation, the indicator stopped suddenly, and I was into a solid half-pound brown. I landed and released the fish and repeated my previous presentation, pumping and teasing the nymph right down the gut of the run. *Wham* again.

For nearly an hour I stood planted in the same spot and hooked brown after brown—all on active retrieves. They weren't wall-hangers, but I took at least two dozen solid adult browns of half a pound or more, plus one of the better tiger trout I've caught in the region. Tiger trout are hybrids of wild brown and brook trout, both of which spawn in the fall. They have the coppery hues of browns, but with the wormlike vermiculations of brook trout across their dorsal surfaces. Locally, tiger trout are rare and almost invariably small. Many veteran anglers in the region have never caught even a small one. But this was the fourth tiger I'd caught on this particular stream in my last two visits, and it was a respectable adult male sporting a bit of a kype. As I brought the tiger trout to hand, I was struck by another oddity: The fish was trailing the head end of a pale, half-digested water snake from its vent.

But to died-in-the-wool dead drifters, the ploy of moving the nymph to stimulate inactive trout is a greater oddity. While it seems counterintuitive to work a nymph actively for inactive trout, a nymph darting or pulsating seductively attracts attention and often triggers aggressive attacks from trout that are not feeding or prowling. I've seen this response so often that moving the nymph has become a key component of my nymphing presentations to inactive fish, unless the water is so cold that trout are in a virtual stupor or so warm that they are stressed. Most times that you encounter inactive trout, however, you're not dealing with extreme temperatures and totally lethargic trout, but with marginal feeding temperatures or natural lulls in feeding activity. These trout remain opportunistic predators even though they've retired to low-energy resting lies and are not actively prowling. Any substantial prey that appears injured or vulnerable rivets the attention of such trout and may well trigger a predatory response.

Predators, from brown trout to timber wolves, are highly attuned to erratic behavior and signs of weakness or vulnerability in potential prey. At least a few times each season, shortly after a chub grabs my fly, a good brown explodes off the bottom and grabs or chases the flashing, darting chub. What were most of those browns doing before I hooked the chub? Lying inactive on bottom, often belly-to-belly with a bunch of smaller trout and baitfish. Many times I've observed big trout doing exactly that. Lesson: Often it's not the proximity of many prey fish that triggers a predatory attack from an inactive trout; it's the erratic behavior of one.

Any potential prey, including a substantial nymph, that behaves erratically or appears wounded or vulnerable may trigger a slashing attack from a predatory fish that is not even particularly interested in feeding at the moment. I've had bass grab bluegills I've hooked, northern pike grab bass, a large Flathead River bull trout grab a whitefish, and a big Madison River brown grab a small rainbow. Trout and other gamefish launching predatory attacks on prey organisms in distress is so common that when I hook a chub in the Driftless Area, I intentionally let it dart and flash through the depths just to see if a good brown moves to the commotion. If a good fish chases or shows itself, I haul the chub out of there and put my nymph or streamer back in the area ASAP. An agitated predator generally remains so at least briefly, and if you get a nymph or streamer right in there and move it erratically, the fish will often rip it, even though your fly may not closely resemble the distressed baitfish that fired the predator up. I've hooked many nice browns by stripping a soft-hackle nymph or Woolly Bugger past a trout that originally chased a chub or shiner.

Time after time, I've caught inactive trout by moving the nymph after dead drifting has failed, as on that May evening I described. I'm fishing the same nymph in plain view of the same inactive trout, but instead of dead drifting passively, the nymph is darting and pulsating seductively, and *wham*—it draws an entirely different reaction from the trout. What is the variable? Movement.

When you think about it, moving the nymph for trout that aren't actively feeding makes perfect sense, because you're appealing to a broad spectrum of behaviors and instincts *beyond* simple hunger. In my experience, predatory aggression is the strongest of these to play to, but there are others.

For one, dominant adult trout are more territorial than most anglers realize. Over the years, I've fished a number of waters where I've learned to recognize individual trout, and I've often observed specific fish driving others out of established territories. This is especially common on lakes or when stream fish are actively patrolling feeding stations. Not surprisingly, a highly territorial trout often responds aggressively to a sizable nymph or streamer invading its bailiwick. On Utah's Green River, I nymphed and released a territorial 20-inch rainbow twice on back-to-back days. How do I know it was the same fish and that it was territorial? Because this rainbow was a distinctive jet black on one side of its tail, and several times I watched it run other trout out of its area.

Even trout that aren't territorial at rest can be highly competitive when potential prey enters the picture. On spring creeks and tailwaters that have high fish densities, it's common to see a dozen or more inactive trout sitting fin-to-fin in a depression the size of a bathtub. While at rest, trout often tolerate very close contact and are all but oblivious to one another, yet a nymph stripped past a pod of inactive fish often generates a competitive response, with several trout peeling out to give chase. I rarely see a group of trout pursuing a dead-drifting nymph, but several hounding a moving nymph is a common sight, especially in the slow-water zones of streams and rivers where inactive fish tend to bunch up. Interestingly, just a few trout from a pod electing to chase a darting nymph, and the subsequent flashing of a hooked fish or two, often ignites a highly competitive response from the entire pod. Suddenly your darting nymph becomes the sole focus of an artificially generated feeding frenzy, and you can stand in one spot and hook trout after trout from the same stirred-up pod by actively moving the nymph.

In lakes, active trout often cruise and feed in loose-knit schools. Many times I've watched stillwater trout race each other to grab a fast-fleeing nymph or scud imitation. Not only does a moving or escaping nymph excite individual cruisers, but it also often triggers a highly competitive response from an entire school.

By actively moving the nymph, you play on another behavioral tendency—you force trout to react faster and more reflexively. They must grab or chase moving prey or miss out on a prime opportunity. Trout in high-gradient streams are often much easier to fool than trout in low-gradient streams, precisely because they must take quickly or go hungry. Likewise, in a given stream, trout stationed in fast water are usually easier to fool than those in slow water. Trout in slow to moderate current simply have more time to study a dead-drifting nymph and reject your nymph pattern or your entire presentation as phony. By moving the nymph, you nullify much of that advantage. You force trout in slow or moderate current to pounce or miss out. And often they pounce.

Moving a substantial nymph can touch off various forms of aggression—predatory, territorial, competitive, reflexive, or opportunistic—even in trout that are inactive and not particularly interested in feeding. And aggressive or agitated trout often move several feet or yards to hit or chase an active nymph. The ability to draw trout substantial distances by moving a sizable nymph is an enormous advantage. Instead of probing meticulously with tightly spaced dead drifts, you can devote a few more active presentations to prospecting a given area. Overall, you can pick up your pace and productively search a lot more water.

PICKING UP YOUR PROSPECTING PACE

I often prospect 3 to 5 miles of water a day, moving the nymph very actively and investing relatively few casts in a given run. That allows me to show the fly to many more trout than I can by methodically searching only a mile of water with tightly spaced dead drifts. Since trout generally respond to a prospecting fly the first time they see it or not at all, covering a lot more water usually translates into many more strikes.

Whether trout are inactive and sitting on bottom or actively prowling, that first prospecting presentation to a given fish is usually the most potent. That's the presentation to which the trout reacts most naturally, most reflexively. Once a trout has already seen the fly, the entire dynamic changes. Multiple presentations to the same fish are like repeatedly yelling, "Boo!" after the first time fails to startle a person (it's possible that someone will jump out of his or her skin on the third or fourth "Boo!" but it's not likely). It's the same with prospecting for trout. As a general rule, you're better off showing the fly once, and then moving along to your next potential victim. Simply put, you'll consistently generate more hookups by effectively probing many stations than by pounding a few. That's especially true on the limited waters of small streams, where trout readily detect a substantial fly on the first presentation, but it also applies to large rivers. Even on big western rivers like the Madison and Green, I often search several miles of water a day on foot, slowing significantly only when I'm working deep water that likely holds numerous fish. By virtue of sheer volume, fishing deep water requires slowing your pace and making more casts, but you can still prospect very efficiently by probing some new water with each cast.

The primary reason that driftboats are so productive for prospecting rivers is that as the boat drifts, the fly automatically probes new water on every cast. Most wading anglers would be well served to take a cue from the driftboat guides and explore a lot more water. Even when trout are highly aggressive, I rarely see a wading angler who is prospecting at anywhere near an optimal clip. In my small-stream guiding, it's extremely difficult to get anglers to pick up their pace and cover more water, even when I know it would pay off with a flurry of aggressive strikes. Most fly fishers move very slowly and fish thoroughly, regardless of conditions. It's the ever so cautious approach to fly fishing that we hear preached all the time. Unfortunately, that mindset usually results in prospecting anglers pounding the same piece of water long after they've passed the point of diminishing returns with a given fly and presentation.

But kicking your prospecting pace into high gear is not simply a matter of altering your mindset. Covering water quickly and efficiently requires accurate casting and making the first presentation to a station count. Before you can run and gun with precision, you have to have the skills to do it. There's a reason why this book is front-loaded with a thorough discussion of firing weighted rigs with significant line speeds and dry-fly accuracy out to substantial ranges. The ability to really sling weighted nymphs is your passport to more active and targeted forms of nymphing.

PROSPECTING SLOW-WATER ZONES EFFICIENTLY

Large slow-water zones represent a major habitat niche. In many streams and rivers, a sizable segment of the trout population lives and feeds full-time in major slow-water zones. Even trout that feed in fast water routinely retreat to relatively slow, deep refuge water to conserve energy between feeding periods. Most of the time, the mother lode of trout in many a stream or river is stacked up in slow-water zones, which is bad news for dead drifters.

Even if the current is sufficient to execute a lengthy dead drift, and often it's not, prospecting high volumes of slow water by dead drifting is extremely tedious and inefficient, which is why so many dead-drift nymphers wind up bypassing long sections of very slow water or barely scratching their potential. Moving the nymph, which is standard operating procedure for prospecting stillwater, shows the nymph to a lot more slow-water trout in a lot less time. In fact, treating slow-water trout as if they were stillwater fish is often a pretty sound approach.

The feeding habits of stillwater trout are fundamentally different from those of fast-water trout. Stillwater trout actively cruise for their food, whereas those in fast water set up on fixed stations and wait for the current to bring their food to them. To feed efficiently, fast-water trout select sheltered feeding stations where they can hold in current with relative ease. They typically set up on current seams, near rocks or wood that deflect current, or tight to the bottom and banks where hydraulic friction slows a thin cushion of water. Fast-water trout don't routinely range far from their chosen feeding stations to intercept small organisms in the drift. Ranging exposes them to considerable current, which burns a lot of energy—and calories ingested must exceed those burned or trout do not thrive. Consequently, fast-water trout normally patrol relatively narrow feeding lanes. That doesn't mean that fast-water trout can't be pulled out of narrow lanes by a substantial and tantalizing mouthful. It does mean that they're not inclined to range far for small dead-drift offerings.

Slow-water trout do not pay the same hefty toll in energy expended when they move several feet or yards to investigate or capture prey, so they frequently do just that. In fact, I often see these fish actively cruising for their food just as stillwater trout do. It's a particularly common sight on big-river back eddies. Slow-water trout do commonly feed from established stations, but they still tend to range farther than those in fast water, particularly when they're feeding opportunistically on scattered organisms in the drift. Trout in all water types tend to sharply limit their ranging when food is abundant, and during a significant hatch, trout in slow water often narrow their feeding lanes to mere inches.

There's another obvious reason why slow-water trout range farther to feed opportunistically: Without the visual distortions and sound-masking effects of fast current, they can detect prey farther away than fast-water trout can. That has behavioral consequences. When food is limited and slow-water trout are feeding opportunistically, detecting prey at a distance and getting there before other hungry trout in the vicinity is important. The tendency of slow-water trout to rush the nymph on detection is something prospecting anglers should learn to exploit.

One of my favorite tactics with slow-water trout is to splat a substantial soft-hackle nymph on the water and then strip it just subsurface. The impact of the fly on flat water grabs the attention of trout from a wide radius, while the bulge produced by stripping it just subsurface provides a highly visible target for charging fish to home in on. The subtle bulge of the nymph is often followed by the more distinct bulge of a trout closing quickly on the fly. Sometimes several impressive bulges converge on the fleeing nymph as trout race each other for the fly. Even dry-fly fishing rarely provides that level of visual stimulation.

When scattered slow-water trout are aggressive and in the mood to chase, you can go on some tremendous tears by stripping a nymph just subsurface. I often strip through 50-yard stretches of slow or slack water while generating a strike or follow on every few casts. In slow water, I usually work my way upstream. Casting upstream and stripping downstream generates a stronger chase response. Also, any plumes of silt I stir up in my wading will slowly disperse downstream through water I've already worked and avoid clouding the water I intend to fish.

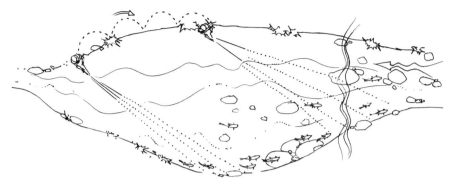

To prospect for active and dispersed trout in extensive slow-water zones, keep your feet planted until you reach the limits of your casting range. Then begin to move upstream just a few yards at a time while continuing to work near the limit of your range. The objective is to work far enough out that you get one clean shot at each aggressive fish while it's still in an undisturbed state.

When prospecting slow water, I usually keep my feet planted as much as possible and fire very long casts. Stripping a nymph just subsurface requires little or no weight, so you can cast the nymph substantial distances, even on light trout tackle. Since you can see and feel these strikes, remove the indicator or run it very high on the leader so it doesn't land on top of fish or reduce casting distance or accuracy. Once you reach the limits of your casting range, you have to move upstream to cover new water. Move upstream just a few yards at a crack and continue working near the limit of your casting range; slow-water zones hold a lot of trout, and you don't want any of them bolting upstream and alarming aggressive fish that haven't seen the nymph yet. Bite off no more than a few yards of new water with each cast. If you cover new water in increments longer than the leader, you'll line and spook slow-water trout that are lurking just subsurface. Be ready to begin stripping the nymph on impact and to set the hook immediately.

In this scenario, most hard-charging strikes come in the first few feet of a retrieve from trout that are seeing the nymph for the first time. I rarely bother to surface strip through water I've already covered. Instead, I make a long cast, strip the nymph through the fresh zone, pick up, and cast again to new water. The objective is to work far enough out that you get one clean shot at each active fish while it's still in an undisturbed state. I've noticed that if I hug one bank and advance in small increments, slow-water trout that are already aware of me often slide off to the side to let me pass or even swim past me to reposition downstream. These may be fish that I've released, missed, disturbed while fighting other fish, or simply weren't active. This leaves those aggressive upstream fish undisturbed.

Slow-water trout spend more time scattered and feeding opportunistically than fast-water trout do, because for slow-water trout, suspending at mid-depths to just subsurface requires little more effort than sitting right on the bottom. Consequently, slow-water trout are more likely to remain on feeding stations and ready to pounce, even when food is not particularly abundant. When the bulk of a stream or river is fishing poorly, I often target slow-water zones and enjoy steady action on trout that are patrolling stations and feeding opportunistically. Many a dog-day afternoon has been spiced up by a flurry of strikes to an active nymph in some long, lazy flat.

Trout often pod up on the bottom in slow water. In fact, fish that feed in current and retire to slow water when they are inactive usually do so. As you approach slow water, the best way to predict whether you'll be dealing with dispersed or podded trout is to consider the size of the area. Extensive slow-water flats are usually used full-time by significant numbers of trout, and as confirmed slow-water feeders, at least some of those trout are likely to be scattered and feeding opportunistically if conditions are at all favorable. If a slow-water zone is compact and close to moving-water feeding stations, it's a good bet that inactive trout that have dropped into the slow water will be podded on the bottom.

Once you locate a pod of slow-water trout sitting on the bottom, dead drifting with a small, imitative nymph can again be successful, even if the current is barely creeping. You're not truly prospecting for fish anymore; you've found a pod of inactive trout and are making short drifts to a very targeted area, experimenting with presentations to see what might generate a flurry of strikes. One of my most productive presentations for lethargic or frightened trout podded in very slow water is dead drifting a tiny micronymph on a slow creep at the exact level of the fish.

At times, slow-water trout are somewhat aggressive, but not aggressive enough to chase a nymph stripped near the surface. Then I usually search deep with a sizable attractor nymph, moving it just fast enough to keep it off the bottom as I probe new water or some new piece of structure with each presentation. When I'm moving along at a steady clip and hook a trout in relatively deep, slow refuge water where I can't see the bottom, I always slam on the brakes and try to replicate my presentation precisely at least a few times. I may very well have contacted a pod sitting in a confined slot, and I may have to put the nymph right into it to generate a flurry of strikes. If you keep your feet planted as you play and release a fish, it's much easier to repeat your previous presentation exactly, and you're less likely to spook

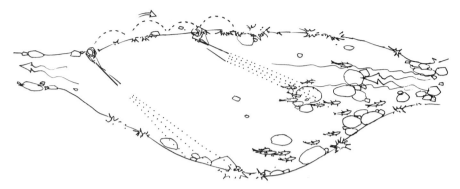

To prospect for inactive trout that are podded on the bottom in extensive slow-water zones, keep your feet planted until you reach the limits of your casting range. Then begin to move upstream just a few yards at a time while continuing to work near the limit of your range. Once you get a strike, slam on the brakes and replicate your presentation precisely several times. You may have contacted a pod of trout sitting in a confined slot.

other fish in the area. Whenever you hook a slow-water trout that could be part of a pod, don't move your feet unless it's a particularly good fish that forces you to move in order to land it.

SLOWING THE NYMPH IN FAST WATER

It seems counterintuitive that actively moving the nymph can slow it down. But when you swing or strip a nymph across current, its downstream progression becomes slower than the current itself, often considerably slower. How much you are able to slow the nymph varies with many factors, including the angle of your presentation and your skill.

Why slow the nymph? In fast chutes or turbulent pocket water, dead-drifted nymphs, particularly small ones, can pass by feeding stations so rapidly that trout fail to detect them quickly enough to respond. That's one reason why it often takes repeated dead-drift presentations to a fast-water station to elicit a strike, especially with a small nymph. By slowing the nymph, you give fast-water trout more time to detect and respond the first time. That reduces the need for multiple presentations, which allows you to accelerate your prospecting pace and cover water very efficiently.

You can also hang a nymph stationary in small pockets surrounded by quick water. Say you encounter a swift chute with a 4-foot-high boulder sticking a foot above the waterline. You can be certain that everybody dead drifts the obvious fish-holding pocket and seams just downstream from the

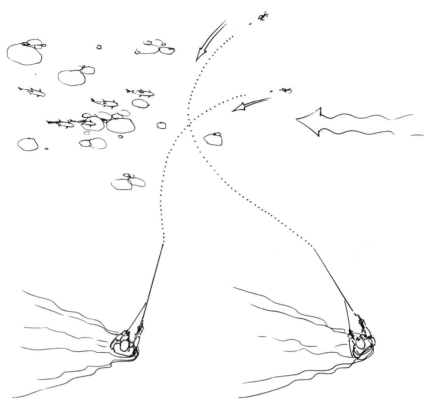

A cross-current strip (left) *or a down-and-across swing* (right) *slows the downstream progression of the nymph relative to the current speed, giving trout in fast or dirty water more time to detect and respond to the nymph.*

boulder, but few anglers realize that tight to the upstream base of the boulder is a compact hydraulic cushion where a single trout can hold and feed quite efficiently. Even anglers who suspect that a good fish is sitting tight to the upstream face of the boulder will have difficulty taking that fish with a conventional dead drift as their nymph shoots quickly through that compact pocket. But from an upstream position, you can easily hang a weighted nymph right there. Cast downstream and across, and then swing the nymph back across the current. Just as the nymph reaches the front of the boulder, kill its cross-current movement by extending the rod tip directly upstream of the rock. As the swing stalls out, your weighted nymph will hang straight downstream on a tight line right at the base of the boulder. Even simpler, from an upstream position, drop a weighted nymph several feet short of the rock, and then give complete slack to let it plummet. As the weighted

Thousands of LUNKER structures have been installed on western Wisconsin trout streams. Large limestone slabs that help to anchor the wooden structure into the bank reveal its precise location.

Eric Osthoff releasing a wild brown trout on a spring creek. On many Wisconsin creeks, the fishing for adult browns in the 12- to 15-inch class is outstanding. With more restrictive harvest, many of these fish would live to grow considerably larger.

From a concealed location in the tailout, a proficient caster can often long-line nymph to distant fish and stations at the head of a sizable pool.

Right-hand casters can long-line nymph through wooded corridors by hugging the left bank and using the stream channel itself as a backcasting lane.

Small, clear spring creeks, like this one in western Wisconsin, often call for precise presentations to small pockets and confined cutbank hideouts. When the water is clear, the sun is bright, and the fish are spooky, the angler who can fire a weighted nymph with near dry-fly accuracy on a fairly long line enjoys a huge advantage.

Nymphing is often terrific as streams begin to clear after storms. Down-and-across presentations slow the downstream progression of the nymph, giving dirty-water trout more time to detect and respond.

Big, dark attractor nymphs, like this black Soft-Hackle Woolly Worm, cut a bold silhouette in dirty water. Adding flash to your attractor nymphs makes them easier for trout to detect.

When lakes are calm, stripping a substantial nymph just subsurface creates a wake that attracts trout from a wide radius.

The author with one of many fine Madison River browns he nymphed in the channels near Ennis. By presenting down-and-across to far banks and prime pockets and moving at a fast clip, wade anglers can prospect with driftboatlike efficiency. On this day, the author prospected some 6 miles of channels.

Trout that live in fertile tailwaters, such as this San Juan River rainbow, gorge on steady streams of small organisms in the drift. Micronymphing is usually the key to steady action between hatches.

This big Montana brook trout hammered the size 8 Mega Scud that's visible in the hook keeper of the rod. Large, flashy attractor scuds tied with buoyant foam underbodies and fished on sinking lines are great for probing rocky lake bottoms with few hang-ups.

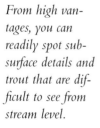

From high vantages, you can readily spot subsurface details and trout that are difficult to see from stream level.

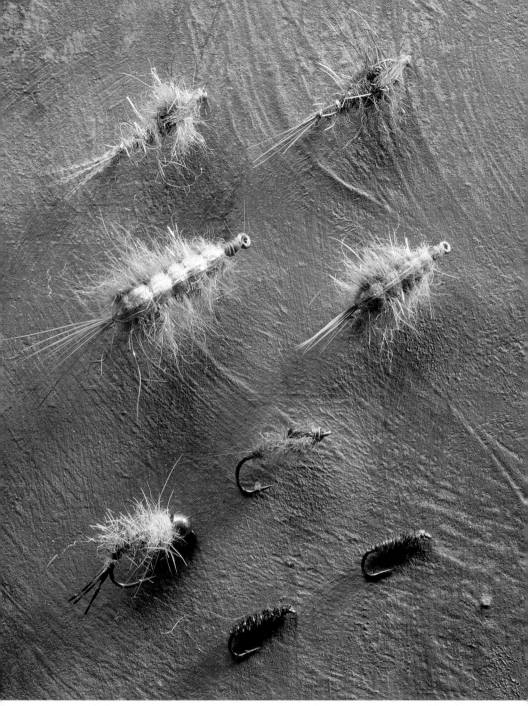

***Top row* (left to right):** *Fuzzy Hare's Ear (natural), Fuzzy Hare's Ear (chocolate).*
Row 2: *Fast-Sinking Scud (orange with flashback), Fast-Sinking Scud (olive).*
Row 3: *Fox Squirrel Beadhead (natural), Floating Nymph (rusty).*
Bottom Row: *Pheasant-Tail Midge (black), Pheasant-Tail Midge (natural).*

Photo by Michael D. Radencich

Top row: *Soft-Hackle Woolly Bugger (black with silver flash), Soft-Hackle Bi-Bugger (black/olive/grizzly with gold flash).*
Middle and bottom rows: *Soft-Hackle Woolly Worms (black and grizzly in assorted sizes and black with orange tail).*

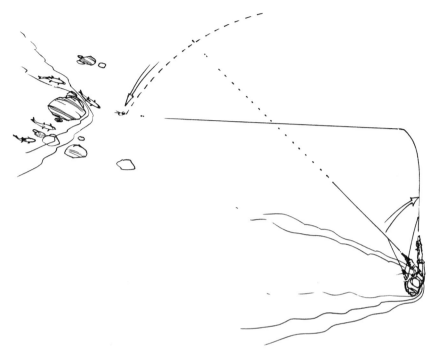

From an upstream position you can easily hang a nymph in a protected pocket surrounded by turbulent water, such as the compact cushion at the upstream base of a big boulder. Cast down and across and swing the nymph back across the current. Just as the nymph reaches the target, kill its cross-current movement by extending the rod tip directly upstream of the target. As the swing stalls out, your nymph will hang almost stationary in the current.

nymph drops into the protected pocket, simply tighten up on the line to hang it there. A little hang time is usually enough for fast-water trout to detect and take your nymph.

SLOWING THE NYMPH IN DIRTY WATER
When streams are clouded with runoff, a dead-drifted nymph can easily pass through limited windows of visibility before trout have time to detect, identify, and respond. And that can happen even at moderate current speeds. A trout attempting to feed in murky current is analogous to a person attempting to drive at high speeds in dense fog—objects appear and pass by so quickly that there is little time for recognition and response. The safe solution to driving in fog is to slow down and allow some extra response time. Likewise, the savvy solution to prospecting dirty water is to

slow the downstream progression of the nymph, giving trout more time to detect and respond.

I'm convinced that moving a nymph helps trout differentiate it against a dirty background. Movement, especially if it's contrary to the direction or speed of the current, catches the eye, and in dirty water, just getting the fly noticed is the biggest challenge.

Nymph design plays an important role in boosting the visibility of your dirty-water presentations. An exceptionally buggy or webby nymph in a dark color maintains a bold silhouette in roiled water. Adding flash to your dirty-water prospecting nymphs, especially strands that are free to undulate in the current and reflect in multiple planes, also helps trout detect them quickly when visibility is limited. Add it all up—controlled movement, a strong nymph silhouette, and some fish-attracting flash—and you can be confident that trout in discolored water see your nymph with ample time to respond.

MOVING THE TROUT

It's standard streamer fishing advice: At the end of a cross-current swing, let the fly hang straight downstream from your position for a few seconds, then make a few short, sharp strips before picking the fly up to cast again. The strike often occurs right at the end of the swing, as the fly hangs straight downstream or begins to dart upstream as if attempting to escape.

Why is that? Are the majority of trout somehow magically located right where so many cross-current swings terminate? Hardly. Many strikes to streamers occur at this point from trout that have been pulled off their normal feeding lies by a substantial and tantalizing offering. They follow the swinging fly and wind up striking as the swing ends or the fly begins to dart upstream.

Substantial nymphs tied with lively materials and fished on cross-current swings and strips pull trout out of their normal feeding lanes, much as streamers do. Exactly how far trout will move to pursue a nymph in current depends on several factors.

Current speed is an important one. The slower the current, the farther trout are likely to range from feeding stations or resting lies in pursuit of prey. Trout in slow to moderate current often trail a buggy and enticing nymph several feet or yards before finally striking or refusing, so I usually employ long swings, keeping the fly in the water and giving trout plenty of opportunity to pursue. On smooth-flowing channels that are narrow enough to cast across, my swings often begin near the deep outside bank and travel entirely across the channel toward the shallow inside one. In

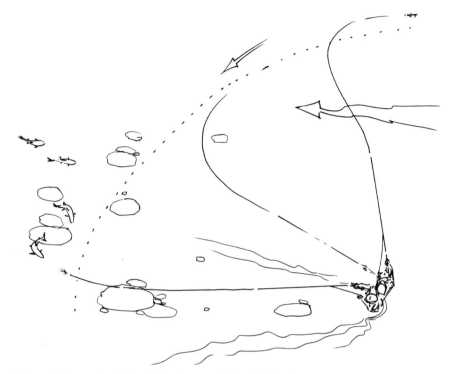

Substantial nymphs tied with lively materials and fished on cross-current swings and strips pull trout out of their normal feeding lanes, much as streamers do. Many strikes occur at the end of swings as the fly hangs straight downstream or begins to move upstream.

moderate current on large rivers, my swings often begin on the far side of prime cuts, troughs, or riffles and move back across current for many yards.

Trout in heavy current usually grab a nymph within a few feet and head back toward protected lies. Consequently, on fast water, I usually employ shorter, more targeted swings, strips, and hangs as I work to very specific zones and stations—a particular boulder face, a swift narrow chute, a specific section of a cutbank, a seam dividing fast water from a protected pocket. Since fast-water presentations are shorter and more targeted, I pepper fast water with a flurry of casts as I cover each potential lie. I often employ erratic movement as soon as the nymph sinks to the desired level and approaches the target zone. Fast-water trout are unlikely to pursue a swinging nymph very far, so you need to grab their attention quickly and motivate them while the nymph is still within comfortable striking distance. Moving the nymph cross-current as it approaches the target also allows you to slow it significantly, giving the fish more opportunity to strike without moving far.

Fast-water trout that relate strongly to physical structure, including cut-banks, boulders, logs, banks, and bottom, typically do not move far to pursue a fly. If your nymph passes prime structure without a strike and you have any doubt whether you probed tightly enough to the structure, deeply enough, or slowly enough, invest another cast or two. Short, targeted fast-water presentations burn very little time and will not significantly slow your overall pace.

The size of the nymph is a major factor in moving trout in current. A substantial fly is much easier for trout to detect at a distance than a small one—and fast-water trout can afford to range farther for larger prey that represents a substantial payoff. So if bigger flies move trout farther, why not just chuck a gigantic Road Kill Special and be done with it? Actually, that's an excellent strategy for probing large, powerful rivers for big trout with a big rod, but that's not the typical trout-fishing scenario. More often than not you're working modest water volumes and a variety of current speeds for trout that are easily spooked, and you can deliver midsize nymphs more precisely and subtly and at greater ranges with light trout rods than you can outsize nymphs or streamers.

When I'm trying to move trout significant distances to the nymph in order to accelerate my pace, I usually knot on an attractor nymph that is large enough to be readily seen and appeal to top-end fish, yet small enough to be presented precisely. Size 12 is my most common prospecting size. On small brooks or on low, clear water, I sometimes search at a fast clip with a size 16 attractor nymph that I can fire accurately on a light rod. If I'm targeting large trout on sizable streams or rivers, or if visibility is limited, I often use a size 8 attractor nymph, along with a 5-weight rod to cast the larger nymph with relative ease.

The aggressiveness of trout at any given moment also dictates how readily they will chase or pursue a nymph in current. Trout are cold-blooded creatures, and as such, their metabolisms and activity levels are largely governed by water temperature. Invigorating water temperatures often move trout out of slow-water refuge areas and onto moving-water feeding stations, even when there is not a hatch or an increase in the amount of food in the drift. Aggressive trout on the prowl when there is not much food in the drift makes for dynamite prospecting conditions, with trout often charging the nymph as soon as it hits the water. Even trout that are podded on bottom rather than dispersed to feeding stations are more likely to move aggressively for a nymph if the water temperature is invigorating.

Water temperature varies widely with the time of day, weather, and season. As such, relative temperature is often more important than actual temperature. For example, trout may be highly charged at 50-degrees F on a March afternoon if water temperature peaked at 45 degrees on the previous day. But those same trout will probably be sluggish at 50 degrees in late April if water temperature peaked at 55 degrees on the previous day. During cold- and cool-water seasons (winter, spring, fall), a bump upward of 5 degrees or more over recent daytime highs usually kicks trout metabolisms into a higher gear and makes fish more willing to move to the fly. If you get a bump of 8 degrees or more over recent daytime highs, which can happen on small streams on unseasonably warm spring days, look for extremely aggressive, hard-charging fish, and pick up your pace to prospect as many stations as possible while favorable temperatures hold.

In fall, winter, and spring, you'll generally see your most aggressive trout from late morning into late afternoon or early evening, after water temperatures have had a chance to bump upward from nightly lows, and before the afternoon sun dips behind hills or canyon walls. From fall through spring, clear evenings usually produce a rapid drop in air and water temperatures, and fish become less energetic and willing to chase. On overcast evenings, the air and water may not cool significantly until dark, and trout often remain quite active well into evening.

In summer, the feeding and prowling patterns of trout flip-flop on waters that warm to stressful temperatures. As the daytime water begins to climb much above 68 degrees, trout often become sluggish from late morning well into evening. At this time of year, the longest window of invigorating temperatures during daylight hours on most waters is from dawn until late morning, about six hours—enough time to cover some serious water before streams heat up. Even on hot days, the water often remains comfortable until late morning. Summer mornings are great for targeting middle to lower watersheds that you know will warm significantly by midday.

In very hot weather, I often target small, cool headwaters from noon on. Headwater streams, with their proximity to spring sources, can stay at optimal feeding temperatures of right around 62 degrees, even on sizzling August afternoons, and their trout often remain aggressive enough to move to a substantial prospecting nymph all day long. Also, as summer wears on, increasing numbers of trout move upstream, seeking cool water. More trout, many of them aggressive fish that are willing to move to the fly through the hot afternoon hours—that's a pretty convincing reason to target cool headwaters when the heat is on.

Rain in any season tends to move water temperature toward the comfort level of trout. Soft spring rains can warm cold streams enough to put trout in the mood to range and chase prey. Summer rains can cool streams a few degrees, washing a smorgasbord of terrestrials into the drift, setting off energetic feeding. In summer, cloud cover helps minimize solar heating and hold down water temperature relative to that of the air, encouraging trout to remain more aggressive and willing to range.

If you're fortunate enough be fishing a large spring creek or tailwater that doesn't heat up in hot weather, you're relatively immune to afternoon slumps in trout activity. In August on the San Juan River in New Mexico, water exits the dam at around 45 degrees, and water temperatures close to the dam vary little from morning to night. Major hatches and spikes in trout activity often occur during the warmest midday hours, when the water finally bumps up a few degrees. Unfortunately, heavy angling traffic from midmorning into evening often makes it impossible to run and gun with active nymphing tactics on some of the most popular and productive sections.

On tailwaters during the busy summer months, it pays to be on the most popular stretches right at daybreak, when few other anglers are around. Water temperatures are close to daytime norms, the trout are thoroughly rested and haven't gorged on a hatch since the previous day, and the lack of competition allows you to roam freely over long stretches, actively probing for aggressive fish. When you're working water that supports several thousand large trout to the mile, prospecting at a steady clip and actively fishing a nymph can produce tremendous action if even a small percentage of those trout are primed to chase and strike aggressively. To me that's much more exciting than standing around in a crowd of anglers and dead drifting to harried fish, which is the standard nymphing scene during bankers' hours near the popular access points.

ACTIVATING NYMPH MATERIALS
Moving a nymph activates soft materials, causing your imitation to pulsate and look strikingly alive, even on slow drifts, swings, or strips, where it's often the movement of the materials, rather than that of the nymph itself, that triggers strikes. Employing and activating soft materials becomes critical as nymph size goes up and presentation slows down.

On slow presentations, trout have the opportunity to really eyeball your offering. The bigger the nymph and the stiffer the materials, the more static and lifeless it will look to wary trout upon close inspection. When trout have the time and inclination to really study a substantial nymph, that's when activating soft, impressionistic materials to create the illusion of moving legs, tails, gill filaments, and body segments often seals the deal. That's also when rigid, anatomically correct nymphs, which look so convincing in shadow boxes and fly domes, usually perform unremarkably.

I often pump the rod tip subtly to activate soft materials without altering the path or depth of a presentation. Raising the tip just an inch or two and then immediately dropping it feeds the line that has been moved right back to the same spot, activating the materials without moving the nymph off course. You can pump subtly while keeping the nymph in close contact with the bottom; while hanging or swinging it tight to boulders, cutbanks, and other structure; or even in the course of a dead drift. In fact, a great way to phase into pumping and become aware of its many benefits is to begin pumping as a matter of habit during the last few feet of conventional dead drifts. Pumping late in a drift often triggers a strike from a trout that is eyeballing the nymph but has not been completely sold for some reason. Pumping as you lift the nymph at the start of the pickup simulates an emerging nymph or larva, which is a powerful strike trigger. (I hook many trout with slow, ascending pumps at the end of both dead drifts and active retrieves.) Also, pumping late in the drift tightens the line preparatory to the pickup, and you'll be surprised at how frequently tightening the line at any point in a drift reveals that a trout has the nymph.

Staccato stripping—pulsing the nymph with short, repetitive strips of barely an inch—can radically activate soft materials without moving your imitation out of thin hydraulic cushions and compact strike zones. If you can seriously agitate fast-water trout without making them move far from their protected stations to grab the nymph, that's a win-win presentation that generates a lot of strikes. Staccato stripping is also a terrific tool in slow water. Any time the nymph is hanging stationary in current or moving very slowly, it will activate the materials, imparting the illusion of life and preventing trout from getting a static look at the nymph. I often staccato strip during pauses in longer strips, just to keep materials activated as I slow the fly.

To move a nymph a significant distance, I usually strip rather than pump. Pumping to move the nymph significant distances puts the rod tip in a high or awkward position from which to strike. Stripping allows me to keep the rod tip low to the water and in relatively direct contact with the nymph, which is a much better position for swimming the fly steadily, detecting takes, and striking.

Strips can be made in all kinds of lengths and tempos. Staccato stripping is just another variation. I do it with minimal hand movement, keeping my hands close together as I open and close my stripping thumb and forefinger rapidly, feeding the line through like a ticker tape. I keep my stripping hand and fingers relaxed, which allows the muscles to be much quicker and more coordinated than if they were tense.

The hand twist is highly touted for moving nymphs very slowly, but staccato stripping can be done in infinitesimal increments that barely move the fly, and those tiny strips can easily be delivered in punctuated pulses to activate soft materials. Staccato stripping is more precise, controlled, and effortless than hand twisting and keeps me in a better position to strike.

ENHANCED STRIKE DETECTION

Actively moving the nymph requires the line to be tight, though not necessarily straight. I often strip a nymph while intentionally allowing the fly line to bow or drag in the current, but to actively move the nymph, you do need tight-line contact with the fly, and a tight line transmits strikes up the line to the rod and your hands. The straighter the line and the faster you're moving the nymph, the more quickly and forcefully a strike is transmitted. On strikes to fast-moving nymphs, many trout hook themselves, but with practice, you'll learn to feel even subtle takes of slow-moving nymphs.

Keeping the rod tip low keeps you in more direct contact with the nymph and puts you in position to strike immediately as you detect subtle resistance. It also puts you in position to set with a dramatic sweep of the rod if you need to move considerable line to drive the hook home. Striking quickly when you feel even subtle resistance is critical. As you detect the take, the trout is feeling unnatural resistance, which means it will release the nymph pronto.

What few anglers appreciate is that fishing the nymph actively on a tight line allows you to see more subsurface strikes. Because a tight line allows you to feel takes, you're not as dependent on watching the indicator and are free to watch the zone around the nymph. When you focus on that area, you will see the take, or some sign of it, with surprising frequency. This allows you to strike immediately—you don't have to wait to feel the take or see the indicator move. You can hit a trout before its senses inform it that your nymph, which looked very alive, is a phony. When you visually detect a subsurface take, your chances of driving the hook home before the trout spits the nymph go way up.

No matter how convincing an artificial nymph looks, the ruse is over quickly once a trout grabs it. But isn't that what strike indicators are for—to telegraph strikes immediately, before trout can reject the nymph? Well, the good news is that you will indeed detect many more takes by dead drifting with an indicator than without one. The bad news is that even with an indicator, many subsurface takes, especially to dead-drifting nymphs, are detected too late. Often there is a delay of a second or more between the take and the indicator actually moving, and that's plenty of time for a trout to expel an artificial nymph.

We're all aware that we've missed a fish when the indicator hangs or darts and we set the hook but feel no resistance. What few nymph fishers appreciate is how frequently trout take and reject a dead-drifting nymph so quickly that the indicator never moves, or moves so subtly that the angler doesn't detect it. How do I know this? I often dead drift at the start of a presentation to sink the nymph and then begin to actively manipulate it as it reaches the desired depth or target zone. And it's amazing how often, as I tighten the line to begin moving the fly, I discover that a trout already has the nymph, which it took during the dead-drift phase with no hint from the indicator. Though indicators are valuable tools, fishing a tight line and watching the zone around the nymph allow you to detect many strikes that you wouldn't notice by simply watching an indicator.

When I'm dead drifting, I usually watch the indicator, unless I'm nymphing to visible trout. But when I'm fishing an active nymph on a tight line, I have the luxury of watching the zone around the nymph at all ranges and in all spotting conditions, and I see takes in off-color water, broken current, low light, and at surprising depths and distances.

One advantage of moving the nymph is that strikes become much more readily observed. A take of a dead-drifting nymph is often accomplished with a slight tipping or a lateral shift by a trout that is all but stationary. Even if you are dead drifting right to visible trout, that kind of subtle take can be difficult to see, especially if glare, wind, silt, or current is limiting your ability to see subsurface details. But a strike to a moving nymph usually involves a moving trout and is much more apparent. Indeed, takes of dead-drifting nymphs are tough or impossible to observe in many kinds of water and lighting conditions, but strikes to moving nymphs are easily seen.

As a moving trout grabs a nymph and abruptly turns back toward its customary feeding station, it transmits a major flash that is highly visible, even in deep or dirty water. That turning flash is a telltale indication that the trout already has the nymph. Once your brain is programmed to recognize that homeward turn, you will begin to strike instinctively without delay and drive the hook home with more consistency.

To me, one of the most visually stimulating moments in fly fishing is the subsurface take and turn of a big trout and the resulting strobelike flash off its broad flanks. Indeed, one of the great allures of fishing nymphs

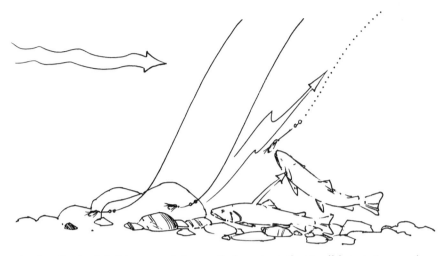

A take of a dead-drifting nymph is usually by a trout that is all but stationary. A strike to a moving nymph usually involves a moving trout, which makes the take much more visible to the angler. Seeing the take, or some sign of the take, allows you to set the hook instantly, before the trout has a chance to reject your imitation. Fishing the nymph actively and watching the zone around the nymph brings much of the visual excitement of dry-fly fishing to nymph fishing.

actively is that it brings to nymphing much of the visual excitement of dry-fly fishing. In many of my nymphing sessions on spring creeks, tailwaters, freestone rivers, spring ponds, and lakes, I see fish take my nymph, or at least some sign of the take, the majority of the time—and that's always a fun way to nymph.

Watching the zone around the nymph makes all the difference when trout charge the imitation on impact and grab it just below the surface or on the drop, which is common when you're prospecting with substantial nymphs to aggressive fish. Strikes that are instantaneous or on the drop aren't telegraphed by the indicator, because as the nymph is dropping, there is still considerable slack in the line, and the indicator doesn't move until this slack is eliminated. A quick subsurface take is usually revealed by a disturbance on the surface. If you watch the area around the fly from the moment of impact, you will often see a bulge or swirl, especially on flat water.

As presentation distance increases, fishing the nymph actively on a tight line and watching the zone around the nymph for visible takes become increasingly important. It's tough to dead drift effectively at long ranges across multiple current lanes and to see subtle movements of distant indicators. Also, it takes longer to transmit hook-setting energy to the nymph on a long strike, so the quicker you detect a take, the more likely it is that a trout will still have the nymph when you set the hook.

By watching the zone around the nymph, you'll often glimpse trout that move toward the fly but don't take for a variety of reasons. Perhaps it's not within their comfortable strike zone, they may see it too late, or the presentation may be a bit too active for their present mood. A follow-up presentation closer to the bottom or structure, or a more deliberate presentation, often takes such fish.

Many times, while prospecting at a fast clip, I've moved a good fish to an active nymph and have wound up hooking that fish on a later visit when it was prowling more aggressively. Like streamers, substantial nymphs fished actively are great locator flies; they have the power to move top-end fish a few feet, revealing their locations, even when those fish are not in the mood to strike. This may not sound like a major advantage, but it can turn out to be. Top-end trout often must be located and worked repeatedly before you can hook and land them.

I keep my eyes peeled particularly for flashes and follows when I'm running and gunning and stripping on those long, slow-water zones that many dead-drift nymphers bypass or prospect inefficiently. A single fish showing to a moving nymph in slow water often divulges the location of a pod or the starting point of productive water, and that's a good time to gear down and begin prospecting more thoroughly.

At night, your only means of detecting subsurface strikes may be by feel. In pitch black conditions, moving the nymph at least minimally to maintain a tight line for detecting strikes is almost mandatory. I find stripping nymphs after dark to be tremendously stimulating. When you can't use your sense of vision, your focus shifts entirely to feeling the take, as it never really does in daylight. And when you feel something subtle and then encounter serious resistance when you set the hook, it's always a thrill. One Fourth of July, I was nymphing after dark on a local spring pond when I barely felt what proved to be a take by a deep-bodied Kamloops rainbow that stretched the tape at 22 inches—a real wall-hanger for that pond.

Fishing stillwater after dark is actually a piece of cake compared with fishing moving water without the benefit of vision. When you can't see a stream in any detail, you are largely dependent on moving the nymph to detect takes and avoid hanging constantly on unseen structure.

PREVENTING HANGUPS

Dead-drift nymphing is at its most efficient on long, uniform flows that have fairly consistent depth and current speed. A uniform flow allows you to fine-tune your indicator setting and weight arrangement to present the nymph in the critical bottom zone over an extended drift. This style of nymphing is in vogue on the spacious runs of many large rivers. Casts are usually made upstream and slightly across current. The rod is raised to control slack as the nymph drifts back toward the angler. As the fly passes by, the angler lowers the rod to feed slack and extend the downstream portion of the dead drift. A presentation that starts a modest 30 feet upstream of the angler and terminates just 20 feet downstream produces an impressive 50-foot dead drift, with the nymph riding the entire time in the productive cushion of slower water near the bottom where the majority of trout station. Accomplishing such long dead drifts with minimal false casting and the nymph probing a slightly new lane each time is a highly efficient form of prospecting spacious runs.

But an awful lot of trout water is not conducive to 50-foot drifts. From the turbulent pockets of high-gradient freestone rivers to the scaled-down cuts, runs, and lies of small streams, much shorter pockets and presentations are the norm. And it's the nature of short pockets that after bottoming out for just a few feet, they begin to shelve upward. If your nymph is weighted sufficiently to dead drift near the bottom through the deepest part of a compact lie, then it's going to snag pretty quickly where the bottom shelves upward unless you either lift it or speed it up.

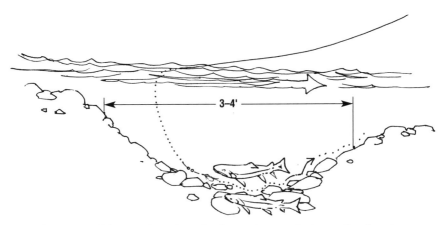

It's the nature of short pockets that after bottoming out for just a few feet, they begin to shelve upward. If your nymph is weighted sufficiently to drop quickly and dead drift near the bottom through the deepest part of a compact lie, then it's going to snag pretty quickly where the bottom shelves upward unless you lift it or actively strip it after a short drift.

And that's precisely what I do on many upstream casts into compact pools, pockets, and lies. After the nymph has dead drifted along the bottom through the deepest zone, I begin to strip or lift to suspend it just off the bottom as I cover the shallower tail of the pocket. That allows me to fish the entire productive zone and gives trout in compact pockets more opportunity to actively pursue the imitation. Moving the nymph from mid-pocket to tailout extends the presentation beyond the point where the fly would normally hang, and this often agitates trout into striking as it teeters on the verge of escaping. During the active portion of the presentation, you can swing or strip the nymph cross-current to slow its downstream progression as the tailout current begins to accelerate.

I routinely cast a weighted nymph upstream of a pocket and strip through shallow water where it would otherwise hang, and then let it plummet at the very head of the pocket. That's a bread-and-butter prospecting presentation wherever depth shelves off quickly. Once you're comfortable slinging heavy payloads, you'll discover that intentionally overweighting the tippet sinks the nymph quickly to trout sitting tight to sudden drops and other current breaks.

Moving the nymph also allows you to probe tightly to vertical structures, such as banks and snags, without hanging. As your nymph drifts toward snags, big boulders, or deep undercuts, there comes a point where, short of picking up the fly, you have to hang it stationary or slide it cross-current to prevent snagging the structure. How precisely you can hang or slide the nymph determines how closely you can probe vertical structure.

Natural prey is not tethered to tippets; it is free to infiltrate snags and undercuts, which makes it largely unnecessary for trout to venture out to forage; that's how most big trout buried in nasty structure got that way. Getting your artificial nymph right into structure and then back out cleanly is one of those knacks that blurs the border between skill and art. To do it consistently, you have to read the structure and current correctly down to the fine-print level and control the path of the nymph both horizontally and vertically. I'm always looking to drift my nymph deeper into or farther back under structure than most other anglers do. That costs me some flies, but I always pack a couple dozen of my favorite prospecting nymphs in anticipation of hanging some where I can't retrieve them. From time to time, the payoff for getting the imitation right into structure is a vicious strike.

Hooking a big trout in structure is one thing; hauling it out is another. There is always that heart-in-the-throat moment early in the battle when you have to pull in the opposite direction and pray. When you are fishing nymphs actively on tight-line swings and hangs, you can often get away with heavier tippets than you can when dead drifting. Those heavier tippets, combined with substantial hooks, give you a fighting chance to leverage big trout away from tippet-eating structure and into open water.

Trout love cutbanks because they provide all-day shade and secure overhead cover, plus hydraulic cushioning in three planes—a floor, ceiling, and wall. Prime cutbanks are often the preferred full-time lies of dominant fish that rest in the easy holding water up under the bank and feed on the steady stream of chow that drifts under or just off the bank. When these trout are inactive, they typically tuck well back under natural or artificial cutbanks into the slowest current. A combined dead drift–active presentation is perfect for putting the nymph deep in under the bank and getting it back out without hanging. A dead drift combined with a slack-line presentation allows the current at the upstream end of a cutbank to grab and sweep the nymph under the bank. Subtly activating the nymph from mid-presentation onward keeps it suspended and moving as three-sided friction builds and the current under the bank slows. As you fine-tune your ability to tease, pump, and strip minimally, you can probe beneath cutbanks for long distances without hanging on the walls or pulling the fly out from under the bank. The longest presentations beneath cutbanks are usually achieved by fishing upstream or up and across.

Major cutbanks are obvious holding and feeding lies, and every angler who comes along takes a crack at them. As I prospect, I'm always on the lookout for small bits of cutbank that are easily overlooked by other anglers but not by enterprising trout. Many of these spots are separated from main feeding or resting areas. I particularly keep an eye peeled for bank cavities in the lower ends of runs just upstream from where tailout current begins to visibly accelerate. Trout that specialize in feeding in shallow tailouts, and quite a few do, often rest by tucking into small cavities in adjacent banks. As you present to these shallow bank hideouts, you often have to move a weighted nymph to prevent it from hanging too quickly.

In dirty water, it's tougher for anglers to see the bottom and other structure. The same down-and-across presentations that slow the downward progression of the nymph and give dirty-water trout more opportunity to detect and respond to the imitation also keep it from hanging solidly on unseen structure. When you do snag on a down-and-across presentation, a simple upstream pull usually frees the fly and continues the swing. That ability to free the nymph easily allows you to probe the bottom tightly.

When I prospect with upstream casts in dirty water, I move the fly to probe for the bottom in controlled increments. I start with an active retrieve that I'm confident keeps the nymph safely above the bottom. If that first presentation comes through without hanging or drawing a strike, I make a second one a foot or so deeper. If that comes through cleanly, I make a third maybe half a foot deeper. One of my first few presentations is likely to cover the productive bottom zone. If I hang solidly on the bottom, I simply wade or walk upstream to pick the fly off the obstruction, then I target new water. By the time I hang bottom, I've already had at least one clean shot through the productive bottom zone anyway.

You can use the same strategy to probe tight to all sorts of vertical structures when visibility is poor. In dirty water, you may be able to just see the top of a boulder, or a surface boil indicating that one is present, but you may not be able to see its shape or dimensions. You can still probe tightly to the boulder by closing in in controlled increments. Before you hang up, you'll achieve a presentation tight to the rock.

At night, a host of advantages accrue to the angler who actively moves the fly. Trout feeding at night rely heavily on sound for locating prey. Stripping the nymph creates fish-attracting sounds and surface bulges for trout to home in on. And big, predatory trout often prowl the shallows after dark to trap minnows up against bars and banks. Stripping a big nymph through the shallows attracts attention and telegraphs strikes while preventing the fly from constantly hanging bottom.

Trout behavior often changes radically as darkness falls. One of the best brook trout lakes I've fished sits high on the Beartooth Plateau of Montana. One shoreline has a shallow, rocky pocket that's about the size of a backyard swimming pool. For trout, the only entry into the pocket is through a narrow strait that connects to the lake. In broad daylight, there is rarely a good trout in the pocket, but at dark, it can suddenly fill up with fat brookies that invade to chase scuds, nymphs, and probably juvenile trout under the cover of darkness, when they feel most secure in the shallows. Fishing that rocky pocket after dark is the closest thing I've ever experienced to chucking a nymph into a hatchery raceway. I'll plunk a scud in there and begin stripping it, and the water just churns as trout race for the fly. Stripping also keeps the nymph off the many rock slabs as my vision completely fades.

Waking a substantial nymph across the surface to attract attention and prevent hangups is a great night tactic on many water types. Spring creek and tailwater trout, which are notorious for keying on tiny organisms in daylight, frequently rip substantial nymphs and streamers as darkness falls.

OVERWEIGHTING

Intentionally overweighting your nymphs allows you to drop them vertically in current and keep them near the bottom during active presentations. Vertical drops in current can be achieved by wrapping extra wire on the hook shank, by mounting beads or cones on your nymphs, with leadcore leaders, or (in theory) with very short leaders and extremely fast-sinking lines. But adding weight to the tippet is by far the most efficient and versatile method of achieving a truly vertical drop in current.

Overweighting is a relative term. It does not necessarily entail casting a string of heavy shot. Dropping a small Hare's Ear vertically in moderate current may require a pair of size 6 shot, and dropping a big stonefly nymph vertically in fast current may require several BB shot. Nymph size, tippet length, tippet diameter, depth, current speed, and presentation all influence sink rate and figure into the weighting equation. That said, rather than getting too fine, I often overweight sufficiently to drop the nymph like a stone.

I find overweighting routinely to be a big advantage. Picture an ordinary riffle. What happens where hard bottom suddenly transitions to sand or silt? The riffle shelves off abruptly into a deeper run. Often the transition between riffle and run is a vertical drop of several feet. And where is the easiest place in that transition zone for trout to hold? Tight to that vertical drop. That's where a bunch of trout can sit completely shielded from overhead current; it's equivalent to you or I ducking behind a wall to get out of high winds. Sinking a moderately weighted nymph vertically at the very

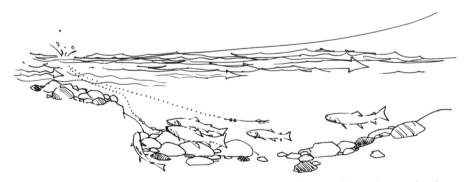

Overweighting the tippet allows you to sink the nymph vertically at the very head of a run, plunge, or pocket. The shorter or more abrupt a pocket is, the more critical it is to sink the nymph quickly to trout holding tight to the current break at the very head of the pocket. A lightly weighted nymph often passes well over the top of trout that are sitting on the bottom.

head of a swift run is often impossible, even with a crisp tuck cast. Surface current extending off the riffle transports the nymph downstream several feet as it sinks. More often than not, you must overweight to drop a nymph vertically in fast water. Overweighting allows you to sink the nymph quickly at the very head of any run, cut, scoop, hole, depression, or pocket. And the shorter or more sudden a pocket is, the more important it is to get the nymph down quickly to trout holding tight to the current break at the head.

In turbulent pocket water, you often need an overweighted nymph plus the right presentation to sink it quickly. A short-range tuck cast with a high rod stop helps drive the nymph downward through the surface current. Stopping the rod high also allows you to hold most of the fly line off the water to delay the onset of drag. That lets the nymph drop vertically and hang a bit longer in protected cushions. On broken water, take advantage of the fact that it's difficult for trout to see up through the surface and spot you. Get close. Tuck cast. Overweight your nymphs. Work with minimal fly line on the water. That combination will give you the most vertical drops for probing compact pockets in fast water.

One of the huge advantages of overweighting is that it lets you deliver the nymph relatively close to the target zone, which simplifies presentations. Say you spot a trout sitting on the bottom in a riffle 20 feet straight upstream of your position. A simple reach cast that drops an overweighted nymph a couple yards upstream of the trout is all you need. A moderately weighted nymph requires casting farther upstream, putting more line on the water, and combating drag over a longer drift to sink the fly near the bottom as it approaches the trout. The lighter the nymph, the farther upstream it must be delivered to sink to productive depths before it reaches the target zone. An overweighted nymph can be delivered much closer to the target, a big advantage in tight quarters and on conflicting currents. Even on wide open presentations, a fast sink rate eliminates a lot of extraneous drift time and line handling.

Straight upstream presentations have the potential to line and spook a lot of fish, especially if you're fishing a moderately weighted nymph that must be dropped well upstream of the target zone to sink to a productive level. With an overweighted nymph, you can cast straight upstream and drop the nymph just above the target zone while laying just the leader, rather than the fly line, over the fish. That's my standard tactic to minimize lining trout when I'm forced to nymph straight upstream. I overweight for a quick vertical drop into the bottom zone, and I bite off just a few feet of new water with each cast. That way I never lay the fly line over a trout that

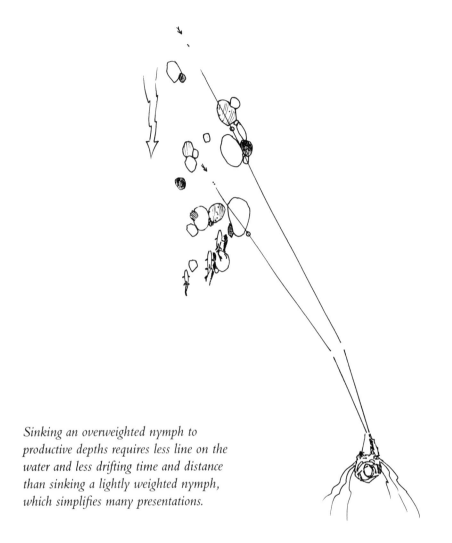

Sinking an overweighted nymph to
productive depths requires less line on the
water and less drifting time and distance
than sinking a lightly weighted nymph,
which simplifies many presentations.

hasn't already had a crack at my nymph. It's the nature of small-stream fishing that many casts must be made sharply upstream. On a narrow stream,
you simply have fewer opportunities to fish cross-current without looming
over trout. If a small stream has overgrown banks that force you into the
water, you're pretty much limited to working straight upstream, because
you'll silt the entire channel ahead of you if you wade and work downstream. You can often connect with spooky spring-creek browns by
prospecting straight upstream with overweighted nymphs using the longest
leader that will deliver the rig accurately.

On sizable streams and rivers, I often fire an overweighted nymph across current and tight to deep, fast outside banks. Typically, I let the nymph plummet close to the bottom before I tighten up on the line and strip the fly a few feet off the bank. Bank-hugging trout often hear an overweighted nymph hit the water, which gives them an opportunity to grab it on the drop. This action suggests extreme vulnerability on the part of potential prey, and many trout find it irresistible. Many trout also hit the nymph as it begins to move off the bank as if escaping into the current.

I often cover long stretches of bank in just that fashion—pitching into the bank, letting an overweighted nymph drop vertically, and then stripping a few feet off the bank. I space my presentations tightly enough that a trout positioned anywhere along the bank has a crack at nailing the nymph on the drop or strip without ranging very far. When casting cross-current to a swift outside bank, I often use an upstream reach or curve cast to position the fly line upstream of the nymph; that buys more time for the nymph to plummet and drift before drag kicks in.

Overweighting and actively fishing the nymph often go hand in hand. Since an overweighted nymph drops quickly through the water column, you must move it relatively soon to prevent hanging bottom, unless you check the fall of the nymph above the bottom with a buoyant indicator. The combination of an overweighted nymph and a buoyant indicator that checks its fall allows for a fast drop at the head of a swift run plus an extended dead drift near the bottom through the heart of the run. This is a super presentation for prospecting long, uniform runs. Following an extended dead drift beneath a buoyant indicator, you still have the option of moving the nymph to extend the presentation where the bottom shelves upward.

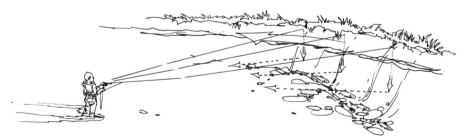

Overweighting allows you to prospect the opposite bank very precisely. Cast across current toward the bank, let the nymph drop vertically, then swing or strip it off the bank toward midstream. Space your presentations tightly enough that any trout holding along the far bank has a crack at nailing the nymph without ranging far.

One of the great beauties of overweighting is that it drops the nymph vertically, not only at the start of the presentation, but also whenever you stop stripping and resume dead drifting. I often employ a sequence of strips or lifts and drops to probe undulating bottom contours or between tightly spaced boulders. In fast water, up-down-up-down probing capability can be achieved only by overweighting to drop the nymph vertically the instant you give slack following each tight-line lift or strip. The faster the water, the more weight you need to drop the nymph vertically into compact target zones.

Up-down-up-down probing is not restricted to irregular bottoms. You can intentionally hop an overweighted nymph directly off flat, clean bottoms to trigger strikes. Hopping is an action that predatory trout and smallmouth bass really respond to. I particularly like to hop overweighted nymphs along snag-free bottoms of sand, silt, or fine gravel. A substantial nymph that's overweighted to kick up silt gets pounded pretty quickly if fish are around to see it. When I'm hopping the nymph directly across a clean bottom, I often slide the shot tight to the hook eye for more precise control.

Overweighting is required for stripping nymphs fast and deep with a floating line. During an energetic strip, the nymph naturally moves upward toward the floating line. If you want to probe actively along the bottom for long stretches, then the nymph or tippet has to be weighted to return quickly to the bottom between strips, lifts, or pumps. The faster you move the nymph, the more weight it takes to keep it deep.

Stripping against current or swinging a nymph down and across on a tight line often causes the fly line and leader to plane upward, so it takes

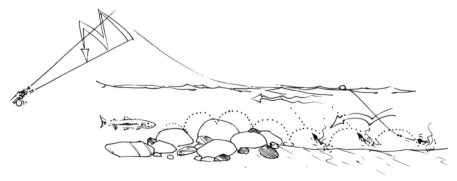

Overweighting drops the nymph vertically whenever you stop stripping, giving you up-down probing capability to hop the nymph off clean bottoms and drop it between visible rocks.

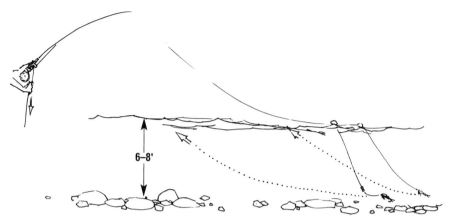

When stripped energetically, a lightly weighted nymph moves upward toward a floating line, while an overweighted nymph remains deep. The more you overweight the nymph, the faster you can strip the nymph and still keep it near the bottom—a big advantage for probing slow runs and flats.

extra weight to keep the nymph near bottom. If an overweighted nymph planes too far off the bottom on a tight-line downstream presentation, draw it upstream a bit and then give complete slack to let it plummet. I often use an overweighted nymph and a series of upstream draws and downstream drops to probe under downed timber.

The combination of a floating line and overweighted nymph is ideal for searching long, deep refuge runs for inactive trout sitting on bottom. If the water is deep or discolored enough to let me get away with it, I eventually fire the longest upstream cast I can muster right across the top of prime holding water. After my overweighted nymph plummets, I strip just fast enough to prevent it from hanging bottom as it moves downstream. The result is a very long presentation with the nymph right down at the level of the trout and the line passing well over the fish.

USING CONTROLLED DRAG

Though drag is usually thought of as something to avoid, controlled drag can be useful. It's *accelerating* drag, ripping the fly downstream at a much faster rate than the current, that looks highly unnatural to trout. Maintaining *consistent* drag throughout a presentation does not unnaturally accelerate the fly. I nymph a lot of trout while using controlled drag on cross-current presentations to direct the path of my strip or help suspend a slow-moving nymph above the bottom in water where it would otherwise snag.

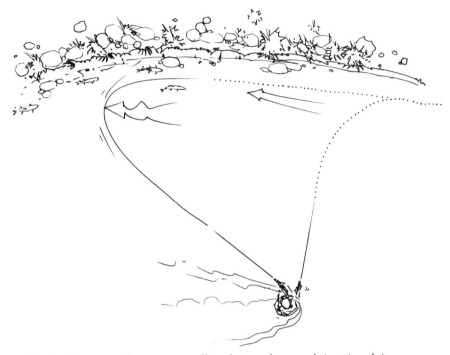

A bowing line exerts downstream pull so that, as the nymph is stripped, it moves downstream toward the bow rather than back across current toward the rod. That allows you to strip a nymph parallel to a far bank or to any current lane from a cross-current position. Once the desired bow is established, stripping speed simply needs to match current speed to maintain a consistent bow and prevent accelerating drag.

I often cast a nymph upstream and across current and allow a controlled amount of drag to develop over a specific portion of the fly line before beginning to strip the nymph downstream. The bowing or dragging portion of the line exerts downstream pull on the nymph. The result? As the nymph is stripped, it moves straight downstream toward the bow in the line rather than back across current toward the rod. The advantages are considerable. You can cast cross-current to a deep, outside bank, and then strip the nymph downstream and parallel to the bank. As long as you maintain a downstream bow in the line, the nymph will continue to follow the bow. You can bow to strip the nymph downstream on any current lane from a cross-current position.

I often use a reach or curve cast to set up the size and location of a downstream bow before the line hits the water. On-the-water mends can also do it. Once the desired bow is established, stripping speed just needs to roughly match current speed to maintain a consistent bow and prevent accelerating drag.

On any presentation that ends in a down-and-across swing, fly speed naturally accelerates as the swing ends and the line straightens downstream. To slow cross-current acceleration through productive zones at the end of a swing, and to avoid moving the fly away from fish too rapidly, feed extra line or manipulate the rod to delay the straightening of the line. As you experiment, you'll discover lots of subtle ways to control the size, location, and duration of the bow on active swings and strips.

A bowing fly line also acts as a strike indicator. Watch the bow itself— that's the portion of the line that hangs most visibly on a take. On deep, slow presentations when my putty indicator and the tip of my floating fly line are submerged, I hook a lot of trout by focusing on the bowed line and then striking at the slightest hesitation. When the line is bowed, you must make a sweeping and energetic set to tighten the line and drive the hook home. That's most easily accomplished by keeping the rod tip low as you strip.

Bowing or dragging the line vertically allows for a longer, deeper presentation. When the tip of a floating fly line and the indicator are submerged, the bowing portion of the line becomes the strike indicator. That's the portion of the fly line that hangs or straightens most visibly on a take.

HEAVY TIPPETS

A 5X tippet has slightly less resistance than a 4X, creating marginally less drag during a dead drift, but the more actively you fish the nymph, the less concerned you need to be with countering subtle drag. It's also true that a lightly weighted nymph sinks marginally faster on a 5X tippet than on a 4X, but weighting has a much greater influence on sink rate than tippet diameter does. An overweighted nymph drops much faster on a 4X tippet, or even a 3X, than a lightly weighted nymph on a 5X.

By overweighting and fishing the nymph actively, you largely negate the need for light tippets. When I'm rigged for fast vertical drops and actively fishing the nymph, I routinely use a size or two larger tippet than when I'm primarily dead drifting. When I'm overweighting and fishing the nymph on down-and-across swings, I find tippet diameter almost irrelevant. If you're swinging a sizable nymph or streamer as you prospect for big trout, you might as well run your tippet on the heavy side. It's not going to hurt your strike rate significantly, and when you do hook a big, strong fish, you'll have a good shot at keeping it out of tippet-eating structure.

With tippets becoming stronger at all sizes, I see many anglers dropping to smaller-diameter tippets than they need for successful presentations. Faster sink rate and less drag are the chief advantages of reducing tippet diameter, but you can accomplish both by lengthening the tippet instead, and that longer, heavier tippet will withstand more bottom-bouncing abrasion and has a much higher breaking strength. I routinely lengthen tippet rather than drop in diameter. These days, I mostly use size 8 to 12 attractor nymphs tethered to 3 to 4 feet of 3X or 4X tippet.

On small streams, top-end trout almost invariably relate to protective structure that they can reach in a heartbeat. Landing a 4-pound brown on a 4X tippet in a small stream is a bigger feat than landing one on 5X or 6X in a wide open river where you can let it run. In fact, a 2-pound brown is touch and go on 4X tippet if you have to stop it dead in its tracks. Even on small creeks, I'm doing more and more of my attractor nymphing with long 3X tippets. If I bust off a 4-pounder on the San Juan River, it's no big deal—one of my next few hookups will be to another trout in that class. But if I bust off a 4-pounder on a local spring creek, there goes one of the best small-stream fish of the season. That fish represents a hefty investment in time and effort, and I want to land it.

I reserve 5X primarily for micronymphing and fishing small drys. Even then, I'm more likely to run several feet of 5X tippet than drop to 6X. I don't dabble in 7X, and if the 6X fell out of my vest, I probably wouldn't miss it until I bumped into trout midging on top.

PROBING MULTIPLE DEPTHS

Overweighting and fishing the nymph actively is the one form of nymphing that allows you to probe throughout the water column in changing depths and current speeds without constantly altering your rig. Overweighting the nymph isn't just for big rivers. In fact, I routinely overweight on small streams, which are essentially big rivers compressed. Both small streams and large rivers have riffles, runs, seams, slicks, tailouts, cutbanks, and honey holes, but on small streams, those features are scaled down and bunched so tightly that a prospecting angler can encounter a different water type every few yards. Small streams, with their fast-changing water types, call for exceptional flexibility. And an overweighted nymph fished actively can be dropped or lifted on command to adjust to changing depth and current speed as you move through a variety of water types at a productive clip, making just a presentation or two to each promising lie.

The ability to probe all depths at controlled speeds is your single biggest tool for determining the activity level and location of the fish. By mixing up the depths and speeds of your presentations and observing how trout respond, you know where and how actively to work the nymph at any given moment. You also know when trout are making the transition from inactive to active, and when it's time to start covering lots of shallower feeding lies and picking off aggressive fish while they are there for the taking.

Dominant fish often take over secure refuge lies that are also excellent places to chow down. Consequently, when a trout population transitions from inactive to active, the really dominant trout often stay deep and become quite territorial, while subordinate trout disperse to shallower feeding lies. To enjoy fast action, you want to nymph the shallow lies, but you also want to nymph the deep lies to avoid bypassing the biggest trout right when they are most active and vulnerable.

PRECISE STEERING AND MANIPULATION

A dead-drifting nymph is doing just that—dead drifting with the current. Once you've delivered the cast, you can manipulate slack line to extend a dead drift, but you can't do a thing to reposition the fly without tightening up on the line and physically moving it, in which case you are no longer dead drifting, but moving the nymph actively.

By tightening up on the line and physically moving the nymph, you gain precise manual control over its path and speed. You can swing, pump, strip, tease, drift, drop, and lift over the path of your choosing. You can accelerate the nymph to keep it from hanging bottom or slow it to drop it vertically.

In a nutshell, by actively moving the nymph and strategically using a variety of presentation angles, you can probe structure and current lanes with a degree of control that dead drifting alone does not allow. Precise manipulation is a pretty convincing reason to fish the nymph actively as you prospect through a variety of depths and current speeds, probing all kinds of trout-holding structures.

IMITATIVE NYMPHING

Most anglers don't employ the strategy of moving smaller, more imitative nymphs actively during hatches nearly enough. During mayfly, caddis, and midge hatches, many trout, including some of the biggest, often key on emerging nymphs and pupae as they rise through the water column.

Most emerging insects ascend to the surface by buoying or swimming. Some emergers dead drift downstream a considerable distance as they slowly ascend, but many others buoy or swim upward quite fast. To imitate a rapidly ascending insect, you must physically lift a submerged fly or swing it so that it planes upward with the current as the swing terminates and the line tightens.

Overweighting to put an emerging nymph or pupal imitation down very quickly, and then lifting the fly, allows you to precisely imitate many ascending insects. I often employ rhythmic twitches of the rod tip or subtle staccato strips as I lift. Since overweighting eliminates the need for a long drift to sink the nymph, you can deliver it just upstream of visible fish and then lift immediately. In fact, you can lift anytime: as the nymph first begins to drift downstream toward you, as it drifts past you, or after it has passed you. You can even lift and drop an overweighted nymph repeatedly. Anytime you are primarily dead drifting and start getting a disproportionately high percentage of hits as you lift your nymph or emerger at the end of the drift, it's time to reduce your drifting and maximize your lifting. Overweighting during emergences allows you to lift precisely and repeatedly while presenting to fish that are stationed upstream, downstream, or across current.

A floating line and weighted nymph combination is ideal for imitating an ascending insect on a long presentation in slow or slack water where current is not sufficient to plane the line and nymph upward. Simply strip to make your weighted nymph ascend toward your floating line.

As trout energetically pursue ascending insects, their own momentum sometimes carries them partially or entirely above the surface. Splashy rises and trout occasionally vaulting out of the water indicate that they are working rapidly ascending emergers as they rise through the water col-

Overweighting the tippet allows you to lift and drop an emerging nymph or pupal imitation repeatedly in the course of a single drift on any angle of presentation—upstream, downstream, or across. That's a big advantage when trout are keying on ascending emergers.

umn. Only backs or tails breaking the surface mean that the fish are feeding on emergers just subsurface. Snouts appearing regularly show that trout are taking emergers right in the surface film or freshly emerged adults on the surface.

The heavier the hatch, the narrower the feeding lanes of the trout become. I even see this phenomenon on lakes as cruising trout that are rising at 30-foot intervals begin rising at much shorter intervals, eventually wallowing in small circles as they gulp from thick rafts of emerging insects. When trout stationed in current are feeding rhythmically on heavy hatches, don't expect them to stray out of narrow feeding lines to take your imitation; since they don't have to, they probably won't. And don't be discouraged if trout don't take your fly over the course of several casts that seem to be right on the money. You may be doing everything right, but if you are competing against squadrons of naturals, your number may just not have come up yet. As long as a fish continues to work naturals steadily and is not put down by my offerings, and I believe my imitation is in the ballpark, I often continue to cover that fish with the same fly until it selects my imitation. Whether trout are working a hatch on top or subsurface, closely observing the feeding rhythm of a particular trout and presenting your fly right on rhythm will produce more hookups with fewer casts or fly changes.

During the peak of a hatch, many trout feed just subsurface on emergers that are struggling to break through the surface tension. Fishing a nymph or emerger just under the surface requires little or no weighting of the fly or tippet. To achieve a bit of sink without adding even a tiny microshot to my tippet, I often shove a nymph or emerger into the stream bottom and knead the fly between my fingers to work out air pockets, completely saturate the materials, and weight it with a bit of sediment. This is a great tactic anytime you tie on a fresh nymph, big or small, that you need to sink with minimal weight on the first presentation.

Bracketing hatches with active nymphing tactics can be very productive. If I'm seeing daily hatches of blue-winged olives, for example, I like to head for prime hatch water an hour or two before the main event and work slender, swimming mayfly nymph imitations actively just over rocks and weeds. As a hatch is gearing up, quite a few trout feed near the bottom on that first wave of active nymphs. Often you can catch a bunch of trout by working an emerger imitation near bottom long before a hatch even becomes apparent.

You can also bracket the back end of hatches, again by working an imitative nymph subsurface. As a hatch fizzles, many trout vacate relatively shallow and exposed feeding stations to return to deeper, more secure water. Working an imitative nymph actively through the deeper zones often provokes strikes for a good hour after the corresponding duns have largely vanished and rising activity has pretty much shut down.

When you are locked in on the timing of a hatch, bracketing by fishing a nymph actively at both ends is the way to really milk it. When trout do begin feeding on duns, you are positioned on productive water right from the start of the prime dry-fly fishing. I often start off by nymphing, and then switch to a dry during the peak of the hatch, when I'm seeing snouts regularly.

On spring creeks and tailwaters that have extremely high fish densities, I often prospect with very small imitative nymphs, moving them subtly much of the time to attract attention and generate strikes.

SUMMARY OF REASONS TO MOVE THE NYMPH

There are many reasons to fish the nymph actively. For starters, moving the nymph allows you to use both motion and sound to quickly grab the attention of trout from a wide radius. Indeed, substantial attractor nymphs tied with lively materials and fished actively have the power to pull predatory trout out of their normal feeding lanes, much as streamers do. That ability to quickly grab the attention of trout and move them to the nymph allows you to pick up your prospecting pace when trout are responding aggressively and really cover some water. You can even efficiently cover expansive slow-water zones where mother lodes of trout often stack up and dead-drift nymphers bog down.

Though it seems counterintuitive, fishing the nymph actively on a tight line allows you to slow its downstream progression in fast or dirty water, giving trout more opportunity to detect and respond. You can even kill an active swing to hang the nymph in a compact pocket or make upstream draws and downstream plummets as you probe meticulously around downstream structures.

Conversely, stripping the nymph speeds your presentations through slow water, giving trout less time to eyeball and reject your offering. When trout do have the opportunity to really study your nymph, subtly moving it activates the soft materials, causing your imitation to appear to pulsate and look strikingly alive. With practice, you'll develop the touch to activate soft materials with subtle strips and pumps that do not move the fly out of productive zones.

Fishing the nymph actively on a tight line enhances your ability to feel takes, which frees you to watch the zone around the nymph instead of an indicator. This allows you to see takes at surprising depths and distances, as opportunistic trout move aggressively to substantial attractor nymphs, and set the hook immediately before the trout can spit out the nymph. There's no delay as you wait to feel a strike or for an indicator to move. Fishing an attractor nymph actively and watching the zone around the nymph brings much of the visual excitement of dry-fly fishing to nymphing.

When fishing in dirty water or at night, moving the nymph reduces the chances of hanging on the bottom or boulders in water of unknown depth. It also creates an audible disturbance for trout to home in on.

In many ways, overweighting and actively fishing the nymph go hand in hand. This combination gives you the ability to probe all levels without altering the weight as you move through fast-changing depths and current speeds. If you overweight, you must move the nymph sooner and more frequently to avoid hanging bottom, but it is precisely this dynamic that allows you to actively probe in close contact with changing bottom contours for long distances. Overweighting by no means limits you to fishing deep—you can strip or swing the nymph just subsurface by beginning to move it on impact.

Overweighting the tippet is by far the most efficient and versatile method of putting the nymph deep at the start of a presentation. It enables fast vertical drops along steep cutbanks, where riffles shelve suddenly into runs, in turbulent pocket water, and in the prime holding water at the heads of depressions and pockets. It allows you to deliver the nymph close to the target zone and eliminate extraneous drifting and line handling.

Highly targeted deliveries and fast drops are key to accelerating your prospecting pace.

You can nymph straight upstream and probe the bottom without lining spooky trout if you overweight for a fast vertical drop and bite off new water in short increments. For deep presentations, overweighting keeps the nymph down at the level of the trout, even during an active strip, while the floating fly line passes well above them. It lets you hop the nymph directly off a clean bottom, or lift and drop the fly repeatedly to probe between boulders or imitate ascending emergers.

Stripping while employing controlled drag, bowing the line downstream, allows you to swim the nymph parallel to banks or other current lanes from a distant cross-current position. Manipulating the rod to maintain a downstream bow in the line also delays cross-current acceleration of nymphs at the end of active swings.

Ultimately, it is moving the nymph on a tight line, not dead drifting on a slack line, that gives you precise control over the speed and path of the nymph. If you add to that the ability to deliver weighted payloads right on the money out to considerable distances, you are geared for highly targeted nymphing that will quickly take your prospecting success to new levels.

But doesn't a dead-drifting nymph look more natural to the trout, especially to sophisticated catch-and release trout? More natural than what? A swimming nymph? Swimming is natural behavior for many aquatic organisms. Though accelerating drag looks highly unnatural to trout, swimming organisms do not. Trout prey on many small natural organisms, from free-swimming nymphs to darting scuds, that are self-propelled and are perfectly capable of moving at cross angles to current. And trout often feed very selectively during hatches on ascending nymphs and pupae.

Then there are the larger self-propelled organisms—leeches, crayfish, baitfish, frogs, mice, snakes—that represent a substantial meal to trout and are well worth pursuing energetically. Notably, trout feed opportunistically on most of these larger food forms, and opportunistic feeding is rarely selective feeding. In my experience, it matters little if a substantial and lively prospecting nymph or streamer looks or behaves precisely like anything a trout ate a day, week, or month earlier. What matters in searching for opportunistic trout and moving them significant distances to the fly is that trout see the fly readily, that it looks alive, and that it is substantial enough to warrant chasing yet small enough to be delivered and worked precisely. A substantial and lively impressionistic nymph fished actively possesses all of these vital prospecting attributes. A small, highly imitative nymph fished on an absolute dead drift is wanting on all counts.

Prospecting dead drift with small nymphs has been relatively unproductive for me unless I'm working a zone with a high trout density. Then the tables often turn and dead drifting small nymphs is the hot ticket, especially if the trout are conditioned to gorge on a steady parade of small organisms in the drift, as they are on the most fertile tailwaters. But that's not true prospecting in the sense that you're hunting scattered and opportunistic trout. It's really more similar to matching the hatch in that you know selective fish are right there eyeballing your presentations along with a steady stream of small naturals. At that point, imitation, not attraction, becomes the major consideration.

As for dead drifting nymphs looking more natural to trout than active nymphs, consider this: All kinds of matter, the bulk of it indigestible to trout, drifts with the current. But by and large, only living organisms move even slightly counter to the drift. Movement denotes life and grabs the attention of predatory trout. In true prospecting—when you're just searching the water for opportunistic trout—that's an awfully big card to play.

CHAPTER 4

Downstream Strategies

D ead-drift nymphing tends to foster an upstream mentality, and with good reason: The longest, most productive dead drifts generally start upstream of the angler. But many days, the best nymphing can be had by working the downstream angles and moving the imitation actively. I'm always on the lookout for water types or weather conditions that are conducive to downstream nymphing.

DRIFTING MINUS THE BOAT

By early September one year, the rivers were running low and clear across Montana. The Madison was one of the few rivers in the Yellowstone region with decent flows and good fishing, but the word was out, and anglers and driftboat parties, including a lot of guided ones, were pouring in from the surrounding regions of Wyoming, Idaho, and Montana. I'd enjoyed several days of decent hopper fishing and nymphing on the productive but popular water in the 15 miles below Quake Lake, but I wanted some solitude and the room to prospect at an accelerated pace without bumping into other anglers. The channels section of the Madison near Ennis looked to be largely devoid of float and wade anglers, so that's where I invested my final day on the river.

I spent the entire day wading and fishing downstream with a ripping wind at my back, covering many miles of braided channels in almost complete solitude. And what a day! Trout of all sizes, including many solid adult browns and rainbows, launched on Soft-Hackle Woollies fished very actively. The best brown of the day was a heavy 23-inch buck that was already displaying gorgeous spawning colors, and I landed another brown that was just a bit smaller. I hadn't experienced action like that on the Madison since before whirling disease was discovered.

The Madison from Quake Lake to Ennis has been described as a 50-mile riffle, but where the bottom shelves off a few feet, you'll often find a good fish, especially near banks and in the protected pockets around boulders. The channels around Ennis are relatively shallow and are easy wading compared with upriver, and for much of that day, I was able to fire an overweighted nymph toward banks from midstream positions. My two biggest browns were both hugging the bank in just a few feet of water, and they pursued an overweighted nymph as I stripped it off the bank. Even with high winds buffeting the surface, I consistently saw good fish move to the nymph. I also had many jolting strikes—an indication that trout were grabbing the fly on the run.

That day really illustrated the upside of prospecting downstream on sizable water with a big, active nymph. Without significant competition from other anglers, I was able to probe each promising area with a few casts and keep moving. My overall pace was fast, but my casts were targeted at the prime runs and pockets, and my presentations were slower than the swift current, giving trout ample time to detect and respond to the nymph while it was still within comfortable striking distance. Long sections of channel were too shallow to hold good trout, but by covering a lot of water, an estimated 6 miles, I wound up searching many more undisturbed pockets than I could have in the heavily fished "quality" water upriver, and that added up to a very good day. It was like fishing from a driftboat only better, because I had the ability to blow through shallow, unproductive water, then stop on a dime and probe good-looking stations with controlled presentations.

The nymph was in the point position all day long: On station after station, it was the first thing to reach the trout, ahead of the line or leader. Overweighting gave me the ability to sink it quickly, even on 3X tippet. I'd just drop the nymph a few feet upstream of a pocket and give slack to let it plummet. After the initial drop and drift, I'd actively strip or swing to control its depth, speed, and position as I probed around banks, boulders, vertical drops below riffles, and the occasional deep run. Overall, my presentations were highly targeted, and my pace, which was closer to drifting than wading, was well suited to contacting scattered trout.

Fishing the nymph in the point position, keeping the line off productive water, controlling the fly's speed and path, and staying with a stout tippet all are standard advantages of prospecting with an active nymph with down-and-across and cross-current presentations, and I'm always looking for opportunities to put them into play. If I can wade midstream rock bars and riffles and cast toward protected banks, a situation I encounter fre-

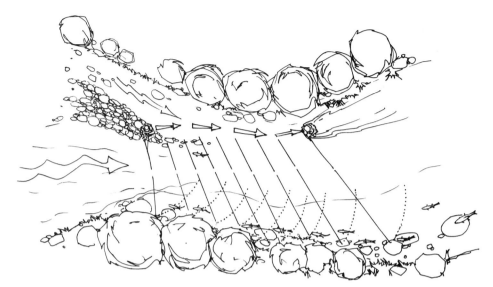

Nymphing in the point position allows the fly to arrive at the fish ahead of the line or leader. By walking rock bars or shallow inside banks and casting down and across toward prime pockets and deeper outside banks, wade anglers can prospect many rivers with great efficiency.

quently on swift western rivers, that's an ideal opportunity to prospect in a downstream direction, blowing through shallows and probing the prime pockets, much like a driftboat angler. Any time I can nymph with that kind of efficiency, the long walk or wade back upstream is usually well worth the effort.

WORKING DOWNSTREAM IN DIRTY WATER

As birthdays go, it was a good one—I got paid to guide and wound up having the really hot fishing all to myself. As luck would have it, my client had to leave in late afternoon. As he drove away, the April sky darkened prematurely and the impending rains cut loose. With the muddy spring landscape already saturated, I figured I had maybe two hours of fabulous nymphing before the stream ran dirt brown.

I began at the top end of a mile-long cow pasture and worked my way downstream, firing an overweighted Soft-Hackle Woolly Worm in black and grizzly, dropping and probing and swinging and hanging. And the nymphing was fabulous. As if a switch had been thrown, the entire stream turned on. Aggressive trout were all over the drink. Even with visibility deteriorating, the trout quickly spotted my lively black nymph and crushed it.

As the water transitioned from clear to colored, I threw caution to the winds and began high-banking—working upright from elevated banks to better see rocks and bottom and the flashing of coppery brown trout grabbing my nymph. Before the water turned to chocolate and the fishing shut down, I released many solid browns, including a 19-inch hen that was a very nice fish for that little stream.

When the water is dirty, the advantages of working an active nymph downstream are enormous. You can swing the nymph cross-current, slowing its downstream progression and giving trout more time to detect and strike it as it moves through windows of limited visibility. In dirty water, the bottom and boulders are often invisible, which means frequent hangups, but downstream hangups are typically benign; a subtle upstream tug usually lifts the nymph a bit, allowing the presentation to continue. That ability to easily free the nymph lets you probe in close contact with the bottom and structure, which becomes critical when visibility is limited and the nymph has to be right down at the level of the trout.

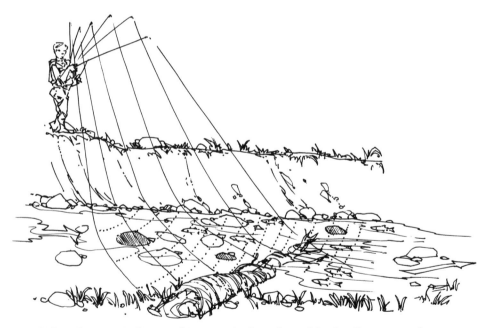

When the water is dirty, working upright from elevated banks allows you to better see rocks, deep slots, and the flash of turning trout as they grab the nymph. In off-color water, use down-and-across presentations to slow the downstream progression of the nymph and give trout more time to detect and respond.

When small streams are running clear, prospecting in a downstream direction is inherently tough. You can't wade without silting the stream ahead of you, and fishing from the banks often leaves you skylined like King Kong. But when the water is dirty, that all changes. Then I like to stand upright on the banks, rather than kneel or wade—often it's the edge I need to spot productive pockets, rocks, and other structure. Also, from an elevated position, I can frequently see the telltale flash of a trout taking my nymph and strike without delay. If I see a dirty-water trout flash to the nymph and miss it, a repeat presentation a bit closer to the bottom or structure is often successful.

Fishing on the front end of storms is often fantastic, with trout typically feeding opportunistically on anything they can grab, but it is short-lived. During a real gully washer, streams can become very muddy in an hour or two, and then the fishing shuts down until the water begins to clear.

I catch a lot of trout by actively nymphing down and across during the clearing period after a major storm. Often that's a much longer and more predictable window of nicely colored water than occurs on the front end of storms. It can take a day or more before most of the fine silt settles out, and prospecting can be hot through that entire clearing period. During floods, trout hunker down in the stream channel; survival, not eating, is the name of the game. By the time the water begins to clear, the fish are hungry and haven't been pestered by anglers for a few days, so they're often aggressive. Hungry and aggressive trout, colored water to conceal your movements, and few other anglers around—this all adds up to a great time to run and gun in a downstream direction with an active nymph.

BUTTONHOOKING

When I'm fishing a small stream in clear conditions, I usually wade upstream to lower my profile and avoid silting the water, but that presents a conundrum when I encounter a very long run. The most active and aggressive trout are likely to be stationed at the upstream end adjacent to the entry riffle, but approaching them from below without disturbing a bunch of less active fish lower in the run is often impossible.

The solution is to get out of the water, swing wide around the entire run, and approach the stream at the entry riffle. Then work the head of the run with down-and-across presentations. This area will likely have sufficient current to provide nice cross-current swings, even if the rest of the run is sluggish. As you fish, stay low and out of the water unless you can step into the very edge of the stream onto firm sand or gravel without silting any productive water downstream. After picking off the most active

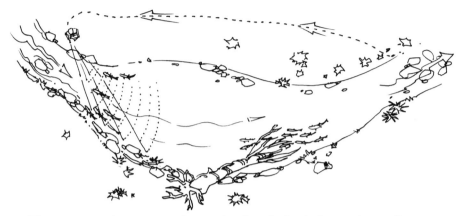

The most aggressive trout are often stationed at the head of a run, but wading upstream to reach them without disturbing less active trout lower in the run is often impossible. The solution is to leave the stream, circle wide, and approach the stream at the entry riffle. That positions you to work down-and-across to the most active trout first, before they are alerted by downstream commotion.

and aggressive trout in the upper run, I often swing wide of the stream and return to prospect upstream through the deeper, slower water.

Buttonhooking does involve some extra walking, but on small streams, those large runs hold the bulk of the trout and warrant the extra effort.

KEEP TO THE SHALLOW SIDE

When traveling in a downstream direction, there are major advantages to wading or walking the shallow inside bend. If you're forced to work from the bank, the inside bank is almost invariably lower than the outside, which lowers your profile. Also, you can usually wade the shallow inside bend without silting the deeper outside bend.

Working from the shallow side of the stream also has major presentation advantages. You can cast an overweighted nymph toward deep banks to achieve fast vertical drops. As you start a cross-current strip or swing, you want the nymph moving toward shallow water; that gives trout from the deepest, most productive water more opportunity to pursue and hammer the fly. I hook a lot of trout shallow on cross-current swings, but most are fish that followed the imitation from deeper water.

Even straightaways often have shallow inside and deep outside current lanes. In fact, there are relatively few points on any stream where a cross section of the channel is perfectly U-shaped. It's the nature of moving water to scour and gouge, and one side of a channel is almost always deeper and more attractive to trout. As you work downstream, stay alert to which is the deep side, and move to the shallow side as far in advance as possible.

When you hook a big trout, the shallow inside bend is where you want to be. You can quickly reposition upstream or down as you leverage the fish toward midstream and away from the hazards of the deep outer bank. When you finally have the fish on a short line, you have better maneuverability and more landing options from the shallow side.

CHAPTER 5

Long-Line Nymphing

When dead-drift nymphing with a short line, also known as high-sticking, the angler wades close to the target area and holds most of the fly line off the water to prevent drag. But many nymphing situations call for firing long casts and working with considerable line on the water.

LONG-LINING FOR ACTIVE TROUT

Inactive trout usually retire to deep, secure refuge water, whereas active trout typically disperse to relatively shallow feeding stations. That's not a hard and fast rule—some refuge lies are also tremendous feeding lies, so trout sometimes rest and eat in the same locations. But in the majority of streams and rivers, many trout move from refuge water to shallower stations when they're actively feeding.

This shift is easily observed on many fisheries. When the trout in a given run are inactive, they're bunched on the bottom, often in the deepest depression. When those same trout are active, they are dispersed throughout the run. Some are feeding at the foot of the entry riffle. Some are stationed shallow over deep water. Some are rising along banks. Some are working the tailout. We all experience it—a stream seems devoid of trout one day, but the next day the fish seem to be everywhere. What gives? On days when trout seem abundant, active fish have dispersed to scattered feeding lies. Trout disperse to shallow feeding stations in response to many factors.

Many hatches originate in well-oxygenated riffles, and trout often invade riffles, or station just below, to work concentrations of emergers close to their sources. In a shallow riffle, a trout can lie in the hydraulic cushion right on the bottom and sip insects on or near the surface merely by tipping upward. Trout stationed in shallow riffles also use fist-size rocks, small depressions, weed edges, irregularities in the banks—any little feature that help buffer the current. When you're scanning riffles in tough spotting conditions, such as low light, gusty winds, or harsh glare, don't just look for hard-to-see fish; look for small features that give trout an additional toehold in current. Often you'll be able to discern trout sitting nearby.

It's important to realize that not all trout stationed shallow are in the shallows. In slow to moderate current, active trout can station high in the water column almost anywhere, including over very deep water. In fast water that is several feet deep, look for active trout stationed high in the water column to be tight to banks or right on the major current seams just below prominent boulders; those are the protected places within fast, deep zones where trout can hold near the surface quite efficiently.

When hopper winds are blowing, big browns often station close to banks in water that barely covers their backs. I particularly observe this movement toward the banks on big rivers. On narrow streams, hoppers can tumble anywhere, but on broad rivers, most are concentrated near banks, and trout seeking them locate accordingly. When nice browns are concentrated near the banks and are inhaling my hopper imitation, I'll actually zone out the middle of a big river and prospect as much bank as possible while prime conditions exist. But usually the hopper fishing isn't quite that hot, and I opt for probing both deep and shallow lies throughout the channel with an attractor nymph. I see a lot of days when a hopper imitation produces okay, but an attractor nymph does better.

Rain increases the amount of aquatic and terrestrial prey in the drift, putting trout on scattered feeding stations. Likewise, low light often increases the activity of microorganisms, which energizes the entire food chain, including trout. Overcast days, the midday sun passing over the rim of a deep canyon, a bluff or mountain prematurely throwing evening shadows on a particular stretch of stream, dusk descending—any form of low light can increase prey activity and shift trout toward shallow lies to feed.

Invigorating water temperatures often send trout to feeding stations, even if there is no corresponding increase in the amount of food in the drift. In spring and autumn, as water temperatures are climbing from frigid overnight lows to warmer midday readings, be alert for that movement. Trout hitting the indicator, scattered riseforms, or trout bolting out of tailouts as you approach all are signs that the fish are becoming more active and are dispersing from deep water.

When trout are patrolling shallow feeding lines, the angler who can stand back and deliver weighted nymphs accurately on a long line can pick runs apart on a station-by-station basis while operating from beyond the

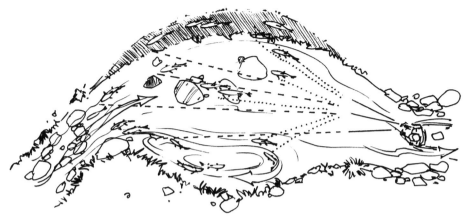

As trout disperse from deep refuge water to shallow feeding lies, the angler who can deliver weighted nymphs accurately on a long line can often pick an entire run apart from a concealed position in the tailout. Cover the closest stations first before targeting distant stations at the head of the run.

radar range of spooky trout. When a couple dozen trout are scattered throughout a run, attempting to wade even the lower portion usually sends a few bolting upstream, riling all the fish. That's especially true on runs with high trout densities. In clear conditions on a run that holds multiple trout, rather than wading, I often nymph its entire length from the tailout, covering the lower and middle stations before targeting the distant stations at the head.

In station-to-station nymphing, as you work from short casts to very long ones to distant stations, you often wind up laying the fly line across the top of water you've already fished. Rather than fishing the nymph all the way back to your position through relatively shallow water that you've already probed, cover just your target station, then make a long-line pickup and cast to the next station. With a long-line pickup, you have sufficient line weight and casting energy to hit another distant station with little or no false casting. Practice and employ the techniques described in chapter 2 for smoothly accelerating your initial backcast right off the water, which is crucial for efficient station-to-station nymphing at long ranges.

Deep-water nymphing is largely a vertical game, with the nymph drifting below the indicator. Shallow-water nymphing is a more horizontal game, with the line, leader, and fly oriented horizontally, much as they are in dry-fly fishing. With the fly line and nymph at nearly the same level, you

In long-line nymphing to shallow stations, the line, leader, and fly are oriented horizontally, much as they are in dry-fly fishing. When nymphing upstream to shallow stations, you need to employ curve casts and reach mends, just as you do in dry-fly fishing, to keep the line off spooky fish and productive water.

need to employ the same curve casts, reach mends, and cross-current presentations that you use when fishing a dry fly to keep the line off trout and productive water.

Long-line nymphing does put a lot of fly line on the water, which can create drag in fairly short order. But with active trout, you're usually targeting specific feeding stations, not attempting long drifts. Even if a dead-drift presentation is the goal, a drift of 5 to 10 feet is usually sufficient to cover an individual station.

When long-line nymphing to specific stations, I let current speed, depth, and angle of presentation largely dictate whether and when I move the fly. If I'm casting upstream and dropping the imitation in quick water, I usually let it drift because I don't want to accelerate its downstream progression; I want a trout on a fast-water station to have ample time to detect and take. If I'm casting upstream and dropping a weighted nymph in slow current or a protected pocket, I often move it early to avoid hanging bottom and activate soft materials to prevent slow-water trout from getting a static look at the fly. On down-and-across presentations, I usually let an overweighted nymph plummet to a productive depth, then move it almost continuously as I manipulate its location, depth, and speed. I often make an upstream curve cast and then strip the nymph across current and across the snouts of trout nosing into the current, while keeping the line well off the fish.

I use both attractor and imitative nymphs when long-line nymphing to feeding stations. When trout are moving aggressively to an attractor nymph, that's what I give them because it allows me to pick up my pace and prospect more water. If I'm long-lining to trout that are feeding selectively on emergers or a steady stream of small items in the drift, then I give them a smaller, more imitative pattern and make repeat presentations to a promising lie or visible fish. It can take a few casts before a trout detects and selects a small nymph. Trout are unlikely to move very far for small, imitative nymphs, so you need to probe each station more thoroughly.

Long-line nymphing to active and dispersed trout puts a premium on your ability to read trout water, anticipate where active fish will station, and cast weighted rigs (a bad long-line delivery often means a bungled fish). It's highly targeted station-to-station nymphing for active trout that often slam the fly on the first presentation, and that's a very fun and productive way to prospect.

LONG-LINE NYMPHING SMALL STREAMS

Don't fall into the prevailing misconception that small streams require only short-range casting. It's usually easier to approach trout on big rivers than it is on small streams, because on rivers you can ordinarily wade deeper to lower your profile. On small streams, this often is not an option, and the smaller water volumes do not mask wading disturbances as well.

In my small-stream guiding, I routinely see situations where trout are right there for the taking, but the angler is dropping a weighted nymph short of where it needs to be, and there is no closer approach to the fish without being detected.

If you want to take your small-stream prospecting to another level, learn to fire weighted nymphs *accurately* at ranges that most anglers can't. Note the emphasis on accuracy. On small streams, with their narrow channels, compressed features, and small target areas, accuracy quickly enters the long-lining equation, often at as little as 30 feet. That may not sound long, but 30 feet can be a long way to cast a weighted nymph very precisely— say tight to the bank on a 3-foot-wide chute.

Few anglers cast weighted nymphs precisely at even moderate distances under fishing conditions. Gusty winds, obstructed casting lanes, overhanging grass, casting from one knee all have a way of derailing accuracy, especially with weighted payloads. And on small streams, if you bungle the first cast to a specific lie, making a second is usually just practice.

If you can deliver weighted rigs dead on at just 30 feet, you'll catch a lot of small-stream trout that most anglers wind up spooking with bad casts or ill-advised attempts to sneak closer. If you can deliver weighted rigs pretty much on the money at 40 to 50 feet, you can consistently work spooky small-stream trout from concealed locations beyond their radar range. If you can deliver weighted rigs with decent accuracy at 60 to 80 feet, you're prepared to milk the major refuge runs where the majority of small-stream trout often stack up.

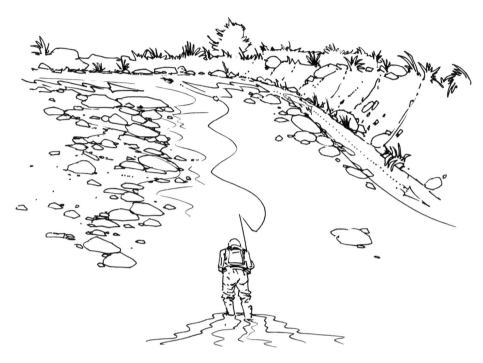

On small streams with narrow channels and small target areas, accuracy quickly enters the long-lining equation. Even 30 feet can be a long way to deliver a nymph precisely—say tight to an undercut bank on a 3-foot-wide chute.

Most of the so-called "small streams" that I fish have major refuge runs at regular intervals—beaver flowages, shady flats gliding along the bases of hills, deep runs scoured by powerful floods. Where extensive refuge water exists on small streams, a lot of trout relate to it. In clear conditions, the ability to nymph those fish-filled runs with a very long line is a critical advantage.

LONG-LINE NYMPHING REFUGE RUNS

On a refuge run, be it on a small stream or a river, there are a lot of eyeballs, ears, and lateral lines to detect you. Often the only way to reach trout in the middle to upper end of a long run without spooking fish lower down is to stay put and lengthen your casts incrementally until you are really airing it out. Some of the longest nymphing I do on moving water is making upstream presentations on long, slow refuge runs where I can't wade or walk the bank without scattering fish.

When trout are highly active, I get a ton of strikes by stripping an attractor nymph downstream with the current and just subsurface over relatively, slow deep water—a zone and a tactic that most nymphers totally ignore. Typically these hits come from active trout that are stationed high in the water column, and if you look carefully, you'll often spot some of them. When I'm stripping just subsurface, I start at close range and work toward the limits of my casting ability, targeting a few yards of new water with each presentation to avoid lining trout stationed just subsurface. After I've stripped through the fresh zone, I make a long-line pickup in order to make my next long cast with minimal false casting.

When I'm nymphing deep on refuge runs, I often work much the same pattern: I stay put and increase my casting distance incrementally, but I usually retrieve the nymph most of the way back downstream to my position. When trout are podded on the bottom, it's common to get repeat strikes in the same location. If I get one strike, I intentionally strip through that zone repeatedly on subsequent presentations. Nymphing deep with a floating line on upstream presentations puts the line and nymph on different levels. A floating line can pass directly over deep trout many times without alarming them. That's different from casting upstream and stripping just subsurface with the line and nymph on pretty much the same level; then the vast majority of strikes are going to come within the first few yards from trout that have not yet been covered by the fly line.

LONG-LINE NYMPHING BIG RIVERS

When big-river trout are active, they typically move out of secure refuge water toward shallow feeding stations, side channels, and banks. Then even big rivers can fish remarkably like small streams. River trout sitting on shallow stations are usually spooky and difficult to approach. When I bump into active river trout on these lies, I often long-line nymph them just as I do active small-stream trout, minimizing my wading, staying well away from the fish, and dedicating long casts to probing specific stations.

Rivers often require extensive wading, but when the trout are active and dispersed to shallow stations, many anglers wind up wading where they should be fishing. When river trout are active, I often nymph from the bank or wade well off and cast toward it. If I have an option, I usually put the sun at my back to reduce glare and improve my chances of spotting trout and takes at a distance. On western rivers, I often scout from hillsides and river terraces 50 to 100 feet above the water to spot good-size trout on shallow stations, then descend to river level and work specific fish. A bird's-eye view is an advantage that the driftboats don't enjoy, and some days on big western rivers, I catch most of my trout by first locating them from above.

Once you're firing weighted rigs with authority, you'll find plenty of opportunity to put your long-line nymphing skills to use for general prospecting on big rivers. I often long-line nymph to probe deep water that can't be approached by wading, especially swift outside banks. With big water, you often have to prospect with long casts across multiple current lanes, which makes dead drifting problematic. Then, activating the nymph to control its depth, speed, and path plays very much to your advantage.

Long-line nymphing to swift, deep river runs can require casting several size BB shot, not lobbing them, but firing them at high speed and shooting line on the delivery. Tuck casting and piling slack line in on top of the delivery help sink the nymph quickly and allow you to minimize your shot string, but to get down and stay down in swift, deep water, you must often overweight the tippet substantially, so work on firing those heavy payloads.

The single biggest strategic difference between nymphing big rivers and small streams is that on rivers, you have many more opportunities to present across current—to cast at up-and-across, straight-across, and down-and-across angles without looming over the fish. When you can fire over-weighted rigs long distances, achieve fast vertical drops, and then manipulate the nymph enticingly on cross-current drifts, swings, and strips, you can prospect even big, brawling freestone efficiently.

LONG-LINE NYMPHING TO ACCELERATE PACE

The ability to nymph with a long line is a key to accelerating your prospecting pace. If you can nymph accurately from 40 or 50 feet out, then you can dispense with a lot of time-consuming stalking. You can move from station to station at a much faster clip than most anglers and show the nymph to many more trout in the course of a day.

Long-line, active nymphing is an invaluable tool for exploring low-density trout water at a fast clip—and if you can do this efficiently, you'll often find rewarding fishing. In this day and age, when most "quality" trout water is privately controlled, remote, or crowded, working neglected low-density areas is a great avenue for finding solitude and unmolested fish. It doesn't take many aggressive trout to provide very worthwhile angling, especially if those trout have been gorging on abundant baitfish and are considerably bigger than average. The key is to hit these waters when trout are aggressive, and cover them fast but effectively, making one highly visible and enticing presentation to each potential lie.

On low-density trout water, the bulk of the trout often are concentrated in scattered zones of relatively good habitat, but finding these zones often involves prospecting miles of marginal water. Long-line, active nymphing at an accelerated pace is a terrific exploring tool, allowing you to travel fast yet probe the best pockets and structure precisely. As you get a feel for how trout are distributed, you can always slow down and work promising habitat more deliberately, but traveling and fishing fast is often the key to locating scattered trout and pockets of good habitat.

If you're looking for high-quality public trout water and genuine solitude, invest in hiking boots. They will put you on far more trout water that sees only a handful of anglers in a week, a month, or a summer than an SUV ever will. My first book, *Fly-Fishing the Rocky Mountain Backcountry*, is full of strategies and destinations gleaned from twenty summers of hiking and fishing wilderness areas throughout the Rockies. Some of the best backcountry waters can be reached only with serious hiking, but many fine waters can be fished on short backpacking trips or day trips by anyone who is willing to walk a few miles beyond developed roads.

Scores of high-country streams and rivers abound with trout that rise willingly to drys, but if big fish are present, you're much more likely to stick them by prospecting subsurface. Two summers ago, I was hiking out of Wyoming's Wind River Range after fishing a group of remote golden trout lakes. Toward evening, I pitched camp on a high fork of the Wind River just a few miles from my car, which I planned to reach the next morning. I had just enough time before dark to rig my 4-weight backup rod and explore the scenic little meadow where I was camped. Small brook trout pounded my Elk Hair Caddis on nearly every cast. Right at dark, while working a major pool, I couldn't shake the nagging suspicion that I was only skimming the surface, so I tied on a Soft-Hackle Woolly Worm, crimped on some shot, and made a few down-and-across swings. On a long-line delivery to the tail of the run, I had a vicious strike. Minutes later, I slid my hand under the bulging belly of a Snake River cutthroat that was pushing 20 inches and would have been a real dandy on the main Snake in Jackson Hole. As I was admiring the cutt, it disgorged a brook trout, which explained quite a bit about how the cutt had achieved its considerable length and girth. Taking a cutt like that on moving water at 10,000 feet was a great wrap to my last day of fishing the backcountry, except that it turned out not to be my last.

While studying the topo map in my tent that night, I spotted a much bigger meadow that was gentle in gradient and well off any developed trail, which heightened my curiosity. Almost certainly the meadow had some more good runs, and I drifted to sleep with visions of big Snake River cutts gorging on small brook trout in complete solitude. The next morning, instead of breaking camp and heading for the trailhead, I left my camp intact and hiked to the big meadow, where I wound up spending the entire day wading and prospecting some 3 miles of gorgeous water. Long, crystalline runs glided over fine gravel substrate. Many dirt banks were naturally undercut, and several impressive pools were scattered through the meadow. Though I didn't see another human footprint on the many sand and gravel bars, the fishing was not automatic. The sun was dazzling on the crystal-clear water, and the good fish were skittish and widely scattered. That day I spotted nearly a dozen good Snake River cutts to 21 inches, and I hooked all but a couple of them on long-line nymphing presentations that kept me well away from the trout.

CHAPTER 6

Micronymphing

The techniques we work out on one water type often transfer well to another. My methods for micronymphing on the spring creeks of Wisconsin clicked immediately on the San Juan River.

After a summer of backpacking in Montana and Wyoming, I drove south across Colorado for my introduction to the famed San Juan tailwater. I arrived on Labor Day afternoon to find the river mobbed with anglers. The scene was a bit disquieting to a fisherman who'd spent most of the summer hiking the backcountry, often without seeing another human for days. I pitched my tent on Navajo Reservoir in a scruffy little site that was a real eyesore after the many sublime wilderness camps I'd enjoyed that summer, but it would do as a place to crash. I had just a few days to fish the San Juan and planned to be on the river from first to last light.

Before wetting a line, I drove the entire 4 miles of special-regulation water below Navajo Dam, checking out the lay of the river and the distribution of anglers from various access points and overlooks. I determined pretty quickly that nearly all were crowded into the inviting riffles and braided channels within 2 miles of the dam, so I headed for flatter, less inviting water about 3 miles below the dam. In late afternoon, I drove up the dirt road on the north side of the river to a small gravel parking lot that held just a single vehicle, which I noticed had Colorado plates.

From the access, I walked upstream toward an immense, smooth-flowing flat that was probably 300 yards long. An angler was standing chest-deep in the lower end of the flat, casting to a sporadic riser. Even from 50 yards away, I could tell from the riseforms that the fish was large. At the tail of the immense flat, the river accelerated into a broad riffle and split around a small island. Below the island and close to my bank, the riffle shelved into a garage-size pocket where I could not see bottom. Compared with the flat water upstream and down, the pocket looked like a trout magnet. I decided to ply it while I watched the angler upstream to see what I might learn. He was a fine caster who looked like he might be a regular on the river.

Since no trout were rising in my pocket, and the local fly shops were pushing mostly tiny nymphs and 6X tippet, I went straight to my bread-and-butter micronymph: my Pheasant-Tail Midge pattern. It's a simple midge pupa imitation tied with proven materials—pheasant tail ribbed with fine copper wire. I rigged with 4 feet of 5X tippet, a buoyant Palsa foam indicator, and a pair of small shot. From the tail of the pocket, it was a modest 40-foot cast to the head. With a bit of tinkering, adding two more small shot and repositioning the indicator a few times, I soon had my micronymph plummeting at the head and then suspending just off the bottom. The fast vertical drop was the key. As soon as I began dropping the nymph deep at the head of the pocket, the strikes started. From my position in the tailout, I took ten beefy rainbows in rapid succession. They probably weighted 30 pounds in aggregate. One 20-inch trout of remarkable girth took to the air repeatedly, hitting the water with resounding thwacks. Eventually I noticed that the angler from the flat had waded to shore and was watching me.

When my pocket cooled down, we chatted. He was from nearby Durango and fished the San Juan frequently. Since he'd worked that pocket shortly before I arrived, he was curious to see how I was operating. I showed him my pattern and how I had overweighted the tippet with four small shot to cut through the current extending off the riffle and drop the nymph at the very head of the pocket. He took a turn with my rod and quickly nymphed a good fish. I gave him some PT Midges, and he tipped me that daily hatches of blue-winged olives were just beginning and that the big flat was a good place to work the hatches in relative solitude. It was an excellent tip. Over the next several days, I had the long flat to myself during blue-wing hatches that started around noon and ran sporadically for several hours. Without other anglers around, I was free to range up and down the flat, stalking widely scattered risers, often from 50 or 100 yards distant, which allowed me to take quite a few good fish on top. Between hatches, the PT Midge continued to click. The daybreak nymphing, when I had free run of the trout-packed riffles upriver, was the most phenomenal fishing of all. I never did see my scruffy little camp again in daylight.

FINE-TUNING DEPTH AND DROP RATE

On exceptionally fertile tailwaters, even big trout become accustomed to grazing on high volumes of small organisms in the subsurface drift, and micronymphing is often the key to steady action between hatches. The best tailwaters have thousands of adult trout to the mile, occupying every available niche—deep pools, slow flats, big back eddies, long riffles, boulder pockets, weed edges, banks. Finding trout is easy. In fact, in very clear tailwaters, it's often possible to observe trout grazing subsurface, their jaws popping and their gums flashing, but hooking these fish consistently on tiny nymphs takes attention to detail. Tailwater trout are harassed by a steady parade of anglers and become extremely adept at identifying flawed presentations. And even if your pattern and presentation are convincing, your micronymph needs to be delivered at the exact level of the fish. You're competing against an abundance of natural food in the drift, and trout will not move far to take your small offering.

For most micronymphing, I suspend the nymph vertically beneath a buoyant indicator, because that allows me to regulate depth precisely. Whether I'm prospecting blindly in a deep slot or nymphing to visible trout in just a few feet of water, I find that presenting a micronymph at the exact level of the fish is usually critical. If I can see trout, or if a zone is so attractive that I know they have to be present, I keep adjusting my indicator depth until I get that initial strike. In tailwaters and fertile spring creeks, numerous trout often hold at the same depth in a given zone, and once I get that first strike in an area, a flurry often follows.

Big tailwaters typically have some huge flats of uniform depth, with trout pretty evenly distributed over large areas. Once you have your nymph riding just above the bottom or weeds, you're set to prospect these spacious flats efficiently with very long presentations. By suspending the nymph vertically beneath the indicator, you can drift it at a fixed depth for 60 or 70 feet, even in current that is barely moving.

Suspending a nymph vertically eliminates all slack between it and the indicator, so the indicator reacts immediately when the nymph is intercepted. I favor Palsa pinch-on foam indicators for micronymphing, because they sit extremely high on the water and wobble at the lightest takes. I can detect subtle takes by stationary trout in slow current sooner with Palsa indicators than with other types.

When fishing with micronymphs and very fine tippets, anglers tend to weight the tippet minimally. But when you're suspending the nymph just above the bottom or weeds, you might as well overweight the tippet for a fast drop into the productive bottom zone. The ten rainbows I hooked on that first big pocket on the San Juan were all sitting on the bottom, very tight to the sudden drop below the riffle. With fast water extending off the riffle, it took four small shot to sink my micronymph vertically right down

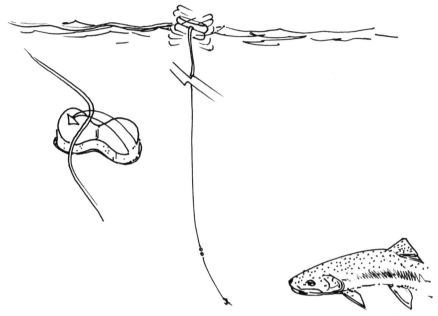

Palsa foam indicators sit flush on the surface and wobble slightly on subtle, slow-speed takes, making them excellent for micronymphing in slow current.

that slope. With just a pair of small shot, my nymph drifted right over the top of those trout and did not reach their level until it was several feet past them. Dropping a micronymph vertically, rather than sinking it 1 foot for every 2 feet of drift, often makes all the difference.

MICRONYMPHING TO VISIBLE PODS

I was speed-scouting a small Wisconsin spring creek, walking the banks at a fast clip and checking out the trout population and size. It was a sunny April morning, and the weed beds that would nearly choke the creek by June were barely in evidence. In the clear little creek, the trout had few places to hide. I could see them and they could definitely see me. That was the whole idea—to tromp the banks for a few hundred yards to see what I could see. I often scout that way on water that is new or that I haven't fished in a while. If I start seeing trout, I can always slow down and fish. If I spook a particularly big fish, then I have it located for another time.

On this particular stroll, I wound up with a couple dozen wild browns zipping upstream ahead of me in full flight—nothing big, but some respectable trout for such a small stream. The fish could not break down-stream without swimming right past me, but they seemed too intimidated to do so and just kept moving up. I herded them upstream through a series of small riffles and shallow cuts. Eventually the trout settled into a 4-foot-deep slot, which for that stream was a major refuge area.

I stepped into the creek below the deep slot to lower my profile and discourage any trout from bolting back downstream. As I waded within a couple rod lengths of the slot, I could see frightened trout darting and milling all over the bottom. When I was rigged for micronymphing, with a 5X tippet, Palsa indicator, pair of small split shot, and size 18 Pheasant-Tail Midge, I stood still for several minutes while the fish settled a bit, then flipped my leader and rig upstream. The trout again milled nervously but didn't bolt. With each subsequent cast, they grew more tolerant of the indicator drifting directly overhead and my minimal casting movements. After several casts and some fine-tuning of the indicator setting, the indicator wobbled almost imperceptibly and I was into a fish. The tempo picked up after that first take, until I was getting a bump on nearly every drift. I stood in place and micronymphed probably two dozen trout. When I finally walked away, I was still getting frequent strikes.

Many times on spring creeks and tailwaters, I've stood in plain view of a pod of trout and micronymphed fish after fish. I've done it during natural lulls in feeding activity; in extreme heat or cold, when trout were lethargic; after inadvertently frightening trout off shallow feeding stations and into deeper water while wading, casting, or playing other fish; and even when I've intentionally herded fish into a refuge slot. Any time I can set up close enough to work to a pod of visible trout sitting on bottom, I like my chances of micronymphing a bunch of them.

Opportunities to nymph to visible fish at close range are more common than most anglers realize. Once trout have retreated to refuge water where they feel secure, they'll often stay put and tolerate your visible presence as long as you don't threaten them too overtly. As you develop a feel for how close is too close, you'll discover that you can often set up just short of flushing a pod and enjoy the considerable advantages of micronymphing precisely to visible fish.

To set up, I ease into position just downstream of a pod. If the trout have already seen me, then I set up as close as I can without blowing them out of their refuge slot. That distance varies with water and lighting conditions, but often it's within two or three rod lengths of the pod. For sure I want to be able to see the location of the pod—that helps put my presentations precisely on target. Preferably I want to be able to observe the reactions of individual trout—that helps me zero in on an effective presentation. And if possible, I want to be able to watch the indicator and the trout simultaneously. If I see a trout on bottom show any sign of a take—a lateral shift, a tip up or down, a flashing turn—I set the hook immediately.

If most of the trout in a refuge slot have already seen you, then you really have nothing to lose by attempting to set up on them. If the trout stay put while you set up in a favorable position, they'll probably tolerate your casting and drifting a small indicator directly over them (and this is required when suspending a nymph vertically). Once you're set up, give the trout a few minutes to acclimate to your form. Even frightened trout that are milling about usually settle down. If you're rigged for fishing some other method, wait until you're into casting position to alter your rig for micronymphing. If the trout stay put as you ease into position, then take the time to rig. Meanwhile, the trout are settling. Once you're rigged and the fish have settled a bit, stay put and keep your casting movements low-key. Don't be overly concerned if the trout are alarmed by your first few presentations and resume milling about. That's common; just stay with it. After several casts, the trout typically begin to settle again. Within a few minutes, they're not likely to associate you with a tiny nymph drifting by their snouts.

You want your nymph to drift at the exact level of the fish through the entire pod. Weight the tippet sufficiently for a vertical drop upstream of the pod, then fine-tune your indicator setting until the nymph is suspending at the trout's level. Once you get that first strike, you're very close to going on

3–5'

In micronymphing to a pod of trout, weight the tippet enough to drop the nymph vertically upstream of the pod. Then fine-tune your indicator depth until the nymph is suspended at the trout's level. This allows you to creep the nymph at a precise depth, even through very slow zones where inactive trout often pod up.

a tear. Don't move your feet unless you must do so to land a strong fish. Stay put, observe every detail of each presentation, and then duplicate any successful one as closely as possible. Many times a specific line of drift triggers multiple strikes, but a slight deviation from that drift is unproductive. When you're fishing to a pod, take your cues from the trout. When something works, replicate it.

When micronymphing in current, I begin with a dead-drift presentation and stay with it until I'm sure that my indicator depth is set precisely. If there is sufficient current to keep the nymph moving, then a dead drift is usually productive. If the current is so sluggish that the rig is barely moving, then I staccato strip in tiny increments, pulsing the nymph downstream through the pod. Lifting a micronymph vertically off the bottom can incite aggressive strikes; as you slowly lift with the rod, try trembling your rod hand, as if you have uncontrollable shakes. The natural tendency is to lift near the end of a presentation, but experiment with lifts early on, while the nymph is still in the center of the pod. A strike during a lift is often visible as a flashing fish grabs the nymph and turns downward.

Once you get a few strikes from a pod, action can pick up quickly. The flashing of a hooked fish or two often generates a competitive response from the entire pod. On fertile spring creeks, you can be dealing with dozens of trout packed into a compact refuge lie. Many times I've had twenty or thirty strikes from a zone the size of a sofa.

Some runs are much more vulnerable to micronymphing than others. I particularly look for fish-packed runs where trout seek refuge in open slots and depressions rather than under banks or other structure. If trout are buried under structure, you can't get a truly vertical presentation with the nymph suspended directly beneath the indicator, which means you can't control depth very precisely.

If you can micronymph a run successfully once, you can usually do it again on return visits. Each time you discover a run with the right combination of characteristics, you have another ace up your sleeve—another spot you can hit for a flurry of action, even when area fishing is slow.

MICRONYMPHING BACK EDDIES AND SLACK WATER

A week on Utah's Green River below Flaming Gorge Reservoir is always an education. The gin-clear river flows through a spectacular sandstone canyon that is loaded with 2-pound and better browns and rainbows. Trout are easily observed from the trail that parallels the first 7 miles of water from the dam to Little Hole. I've walked and fished that entire stretch many times, observing how the trout are distributed and behave. A bird's-eye view

Trout in large eddies often cruise for their food, just as trout do in lakes. By working from a high vantage, such as atop a big boulder, you can often observe cruising trout and drop your micronymph directly in their paths.

of the river makes it quickly apparent that a high percentage of the trout relate to the many large back eddies, which is also common behavior on other big tailwaters.

Many eddy trout actively cruise for their food, just as trout do in lakes, and actively micronymphing to visible eddy cruisers from atop big boulders and other good vantages is similar to sight-fishing on lakes. With a few feet of elevation, you can usually observe several cruisers at once and note their routes, depth, and speed. The name of the game is to lead a cruising trout with your cast and drop your micronymph directly in its path. Trout often spot the nymph on the drop and accelerate a bit to intercept it. If a fish shows no sign of seeing the imitation, then subtly strip to attract attention just as the fish approaches. Often you can make two or three presentations to a trout before it cruises out of view or range. If one of those is directly in the path of the trout, your chance for a hookup is good.

When I can see cruising fish and observe their reactions, I often remove the indicator so that the entire leader is free to sink when I need to get the nymph down several feet. In lazy eddies, it takes only one or two microshot to drop a micronymph a few feet into the path of a cruiser, and a long, slender tippet can enhance the sink rate. Putting the nymph directly into the path of trout is crucial, and to do that consistently, you have to be able to see the fish, which is much easier from an elevated position. Don't worry about eddy cruisers seeing you. Trout circulating over big eddies feel pretty secure. They're not nearly as exposed or spooky as trout sitting in thin water along banks. Heck, eddy cruisers see driftboat anglers pass directly overhead in squadrons, and it barely alters their feeding rhythms. A lone man standing on a rock 50 feet away is not likely to alarm them.

When eddy trout are inactive, they often suspend in slack water in loose-knit pods. To work to these trout, I usually remove the indicator and rig with a single microshot. In the absence of current, this is enough weight to sink a micronymph to trout suspended several feet down. Then I experiment with active retrieves to see what the trout will respond to—staccato strips, subtle pumps, lifts. Working from a good vantage where I can see the trout keeps my nymph right in their midst and allows me to observe their reactions. If I can crack the code on a single eddy, I find that I can usually take good fish on other eddies with the same technique.

On big eddies, it's also common to see several good trout lined along shore in very thin water. The dark forms of the trout are highly visible as they hold over narrow strips of lightly colored sand between shore and weeds. These stationary trout face into the gentle current, which in an eddy has them looking downriver. They are actively feeding and are extremely vulnerable to a micronymph if you approach them strategically

On a large eddy, it's common to see several good trout stationed along the bank in very thin water. Remove the indicator and use a reach cast to drop a micronymph just upstream of each visible fish. Then roll the nymph right along the sand to the fish. If the fish shifts laterally or tips downward, set the hook. Target the last trout in line first. When you hook a trout, steer the fight toward the center of the eddy away from the other fish stationed along the bank. Often you can work right up the line and pick off several good trout in quick succession on the exact same micronymph and presentation.

and cast precisely. Rig with one small shot and remove your indicator. Stay close to the bank, keep low, and wade silently as you approach each trout from the blind spot directly behind it. From a range of 20 or 30 feet, drop the nymph a yard or two above a trout and simply roll it right along the clean sand bottom (use a reach cast to keep your leader butt off the fish). As the nymph rolls with the current, watch for the trout to shift laterally or tip downward. If it does either, set the hook. I once micronymphed five rainbows in quick succession from a single strip of sand, and I saw every one of them tip downward to pick the nymph right off the bottom.

In micronymphing, a subtle adjustment can make your day on trout that are lethargic, spooked, well educated, or just unwilling to move to eat. The more I micronymph, the more variations I find for fooling demanding trout.

CHAPTER 7

No-Line Nymphing

A big box elder had dropped smack across the small pool since my last visit, enhancing its trout-holding potential considerably. I waded quietly on firm sand until I was less than a rod length downstream of the half-submerged trunk. I could see the tail end of what looked to be a nice pocket scoured under the trunk, providing plenty of depth and cover for trout. If a trout was in the pocket, it would be sitting on the bottom only about 6 feet from where I stood, facing into the gentle current.

I was fishing an 8-foot, 4-weight rod with a leader that was a bit shorter than the rod. With only a foot of fly line beyond the rod tip, I raised the rod so that my overweighted nymph hung straight down by my side. Then I made a little elliptical swing and tuck-cast over the trunk. As the nymph dropped into the pocket, I extended the rod and reached right, causing the fly to slide across the current and directly under the trunk on a tight line. I felt a jolt and my rod tip was jerked right down into the water as a powerful trout bored back under the trunk.

I had one chance—I charged upstream and scrambled over the log. From upstream of the tree, I fought the trout on the same short line on which I'd hooked it, with my leader butt barely out of the guides. The trout sat under the log shaking its head violently, but the hook and my 3X tippet were up to snuff. Eventually I tailed a distinctive-looking brown trout that had a pronounced kype and just a few big spots scattered across its broad, coppery flanks. It stretched the tape at 18 inches—an exceptional brown for that little headwater stream and a fitting reward for hanging in there on a scorching August afternoon.

NYMPHING FROM BLIND SPOTS

Trout love overhead cover, which provides shade and security from predators. I've taken good trout under low-slung tractor and snowmobile bridges that sit just a foot or two above the water. Southwestern Wisconsin is dairy country, with a lot of barbed-wire fences crossing the streams. During high water, the bottom strand of wire can collect branches, grass, corn stalks, and other debris and get dragged down permanently into the stream. If there is any depth under the debris, trout will sit under it. Wooded streams, from lodgepole forests to box elder bottoms, are often crisscrossed with downed logs. Current deflecting downward under half-submerged logs often scours compact pockets, creating refuges where trout can both feed and hide. Some treetops and trunks topple across existing pools, turning them into full-blown trout sanctuaries. Root systems sticking out of banks provide over-head cover. Low-growing branches, or sweepers, collect mats of floating debris. Sticks and foam collect in eddy whorls.

Trout sitting directly under these forms of overhead cover and facing upstream have a complete blind spot above and behind. They cannot see you approaching from downstream. If your approach is quiet and you stay just slightly behind the upstream face of the cover, you can set up close enough to fish with just a few feet of leader in the water. I find many opportunities to probe under snags and logs at point-blank range from completely concealed blind spots.

Whether I'm wading or on the bank, I stay just far enough back from the upstream face of overhead cover that a trout looking upstream or straight up could not see me. I make the presentation with only the rod tip

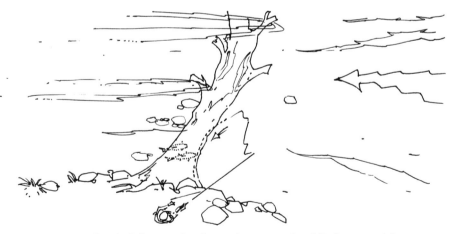

A trout sitting directly below overhead cover has a complete blind spot straight above. If you approach quietly and keep your body slightly behind the upstream face of an obstruction, you can often nymph to trout under logs and other debris at very close range without being seen.

Little serpentine streams with doglegs and sharp curves offer many opportunities to nymph around corners at very close range from totally concealed positions.

appearing in the trout's window of view. I typically overweight the nymph for a fast drop. After the drop, I slide the fly across the current on a tight line so I can feel strikes instantly, set the hook quickly, and check the downstream progression of the nymph before it gets too far into debris. This swings the imitation right across the snouts of trout, agitating the fish and giving them plenty of opportunity to strike.

Casting a weighted rig precisely on just the leader takes a bit of practice, but it really pays off. If my overhead rod space is clear, I raise my rod hand and the rod to the roll-cast position. With the rig and leader hanging straight down from the rod tip, I use a short, elliptical casting stroke. That little elliptical swing puts the rig on a taut line and builds sufficient momentum to tuck on the forward delivery and drive the nymph accurately to the water. I usually make the delivery to the deep side of the cover to set up the cross-current swing, which is controlled mostly by manipulating the rod.

If overhead casting lanes are blocked, then a bow and arrow cast or even dapping can work. One of the best rainbows I've ever taken on a small Wisconsin stream was dapped with not much more than the tippet outside the rod tip. Hookups don't get much more intense than a big, hot rainbow on 3 feet of leader. Light tippets really aren't necessary to get strikes in these situations, and using a 3X or heavier tippet gives you a fighting chance to whip a good fish on a short line. In most cases, you eventually must work the fish upstream to move it out from under overhead cover and land it. Moving upstream of the structure as soon as you hook a good fish gives you more leverage and steering ability.

Little serpentine streams with doglegs and curves offer many opportunities to fish around corners at close range from totally concealed positions. As you're wading upstream and rounding a corner, stay to the inside bend, and take a peek around the corner before you show yourself. If there is good water tight to your bank, you can probe it with a little tuck cast while holding most of the leader off the water.

NO-LINING IN RIFFLES

Broken water blurs and distorts the fish's view of objects above the surface. Moving water also muffles wading disturbances. In riffles and turbulent pocket water, it's often possible to get within 5 to 15 feet of trout and present with just a few feet of leader in the water. On no-line presentations through riffles, I high-stick for the entire drift, holding as much of the leader off the water as possible as I subtly jig an overweighted nymph up and down on a tight leader, dropping it into the deeper cuts and bouncing it off the bottom between lifts. The vertical jigging action grabs the attention of trout, while the tight leader and subtle lifts allow me to instantly feel when a fish grabs the nymph. The jigging can be very subtle—just enough to lift the rig a bit off the bottom and maintain that tight-line contact to detect strikes. When probing riffles at close range, you will often see a flashing tail or flank as a fish takes. On no-line presentations, an indicator positioned on the upper half of the leader is usually suspended in midair, so you're dependent on detecting strikes by feeling or seeing them. If you see a flash but the trout misses the nymph, go right back with a second or third presentation. On short drifts through quick pockets, it's not unusual for trout to miss an active nymph once or twice and then grab it solidly.

I often no-line nymph swift, narrow tailouts by approaching as closely as I can from downstream, then making an upstream flip and extending the

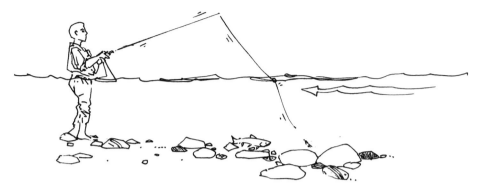

Riffles and turbulent pocket water reduce the ability of trout to see up through the surface. In broken water, it's often possible to nymph trout at very close range with little or no line on the water.

rod to hold all but a few feet of tippet clear of the water. With just a few feet of small-diameter tippet in the water, accelerating drag—the big bugaboo when nymphing tailouts—is largely defeated.

After long-lining the body of a pool or run, I often walk right up to a fast entry chute and no-line with an overweighted nymph and an absolutely vertical presentation that cuts right through the current to the bottom. This gives the nymph more hang time close to the bottom than is possible with fly line on the water. Even if I've really stirred up a pool in the course of fishing it, trout stationed in swift entry chutes and riffles are often oblivious to the nearby commotion. They live in a buffered world, and their range of hearing and ability to see up through the surface are limited. If you're prospecting along at a fast clip and wind up right on top of a swift, little pocket before you realize it's there, just put on the brakes and probe it with a no-line presentation. There's a good chance that trout just a short flip away haven't detected you.

Spring is a particularly good time to fish riffles at close range. Flows are good and many springtime hatches originate in riffles, encouraging trout to move there to feed. The water is usually a bit off-color, which provides you with additional concealment. On warm spring afternoons and evenings, as feeding temperatures bump up to an optimal 55 to 60 degrees for the first time in several months and insect activity picks up, trout are really drawn to riffles.

Fast-water fish usually do not move far to take nymphs. Look for buffered zones within riffles where trout can hold, and then target those prime lies precisely.

NO-LINING IN CLOUDY WATER

Cloudy water provides an extra margin of concealment that can make all the difference. When it begins to rain, or as water is still in the clearing process after storms, I often beeline for streams that are particularly difficult to conquer when they're running crystal clear, and I no-line nymph to my heart's content. Brushy streams with very obstructed casting lanes fall into that category. When the water goes cloudy, I can no-line nymph virtually an entire stream, including many runs that are difficult to get a fly into in clear conditions.

Streams with high densities of trout can turn extremely generous when the water runs cloudy. In clear conditions, the commotion of taking a trout or two usually alerts an entire run. In murky conditions, you can often nymph multiple trout on run after run.

In dirty water, I do a lot of high-banking, especially on pasture streams. Instead of fishing from the shallow inside bend and keeping a low profile, I get right up on top of the deeper outside banks and no-line nymph vertically through the deepest slots, dropping the nymph right on the bottom and then jigging it a bit to attract attention throughout the drift. From the high bank, I can better see the vague outlines of rocks and wood, the bottom, and the trout's flashing takes. With just a few feet of leader in the water, accelerating drag is largely eliminated, and I can achieve excellent hang time near the bottom.

CHAPTER 8

Nymphing Lakes

Most fly fishing on lakes, nymphing or otherwise, revolves around moving the fly. When you're prospecting large volumes of mostly empty water, moving the fly is often essential for locating the limited zones that trout are using and grabbing the fish's attention. When confronted with the tremendous water volume of lakes, most anglers intuitively grasp that there are overwhelming advantages to moving the fly. Nymphing extensively on lakes taught me the many fundamental advantages of moving the nymph, advantages that I now routinely put into play on moving waters.

Nymphing lakes teaches you to double haul weighted nymphs smoothly. Casting distances tend to be long. Opportunities at visible cruisers tend to be fleeting. And the wind often blows completely unfettered. To nymph lakes effectively, you must be able to buck the wind and deliver weighted nymphs on long lines.

Most nymphing on lakes is performed without an indicator. That develops your ability to feel subsurface takes on all kinds of active retrieves, from energetic strips to slow crawls. Fishing lakes also hones your scouting ability. You simply can't explore reams and reams of water by fishing it all. You have to use your head, eyes, and mobility to zero in on productive water.

Casting weighted rigs with authority, detecting strikes by feel, scouting and prospecting efficiently—all are vital skills for fishing the nymph actively on moving water, and fishing lakes is a great place to acquire them.

Fishing lakes is also its own reward. The trout usually grow larger than in neighboring streams and rivers. Competition from other anglers is often nil. And trout lakes tend to sit in compelling country. Anglers armed with a few potent nymphing techniques can have a lot of absorbing and rewarding fishing pretty much to themselves.

NYMPHING TO VISIBLE CRUISERS

By the time I made my first trek into Lightning Lake in the Beartooth Mountains of Montana, I'd already caught many large golden trout in the Wind River Range of Wyoming, including several fish in the 24-inch class that were pushing 6 pounds. Then Lightning started kicking out Montana state-record goldens in the 4-pound range, and a Fish and Game crew reportedly gill-netted a 10-pounder. Any golden lake in that class I had to see for myself.

I hiked into Lightning the scenic way—over the top of Chalice Peak. I descended to the lake in late evening with just enough time to make camp. It was after Labor Day, and another high-country summer was winding down. I awoke my first morning on Lightning to a hard frost and ice in my water bottle, but I rolled out early to start exploring a couple miles of ragged and unfamiliar shoreline. The shallows were cold and shaded, and I scouted more than halfway around the lake without seeing a fish. I followed the outlet stream down to Little Lightning Lake, where I saw a lot of small goldens. By the time I returned to the big lake, the sun had climbed and the day was warming nicely. Spotting conditions had also improved.

Lightning was too big to start prospecting blindly so early in the game, so I decided to watch a promising rock flat I'd located earlier. That turned out to be a fortunate move. I'd just hopped atop a big boulder for a better vantage of the flat when I saw a cruiser crossing directly in front of me about 50 feet out. The trout was close to the bottom in maybe 8 feet of water and moving fast. I'd get only one shot. I dropped a Fast-Sinking Scud some 20 feet ahead of the trout. The fish accelerated and then stopped in the vicinity of the sinking fly. I didn't see or feel a take, but I knew from experience that when a golden slammed on the brakes near a dropping fly, it probably had taken it. I set the hook. The big golden zipped toward the middle of the lake, jumping and ripping up the surface. Then it dived. It was several minutes before I recovered even my backing. That powerful golden wound up stretching the tape at 21 inches and easily would have topped 4 pounds—a potential state-record fish on my very first hookup. I snapped a few photos of the fish in the water next to my rod and turned it loose. A few minutes later, from atop the same boulder, I spotted and caught another golden that was almost as large. I was beginning to like Lightning Lake.

Catching trophy trout near or above timberline often requires considerable legwork. Many of my favorite lakes require round-trip hikes of 30 to 70 miles. High lakes with big, healthy trout usually have very low fish densities, so even after you arrive at a lake, your legs and polarized glasses remain your most valuable prospecting tools. One of my first orders of business on any high lake is to walk the shoreline and locate the prime food-producing shallows as I simultaneously scan for cruising fish. Scuds (common at all elevations) and fairy shrimp (common at high altitudes) are the primary forage on many trophy lake fisheries. Fairy shrimp are easily distinguished from scuds: The shrimp are softer and more transparent, and they swim on their backs with their soft legs and gill filaments undulating upward from their sides. Midges are often abundant, and mayflies, caddis, and stoneflies are usually present to varying degrees. Most crustaceans and aquatic insects inhabit the shallow zones, not the depths. On alpine lakes, trout sometimes vanish into the depths to feed on plankton, especially in late summer during warm weather, but even then some fish usually cruise the shallows for more substantial prey for at least part of the day. Observing the primary feeding flats and sight-fishing to cruisers can be very productive, even if you wind up looking for fish most of the time and fishing very little. When you're sight-casting to trophy fish, it takes only a few well-executed casts to make for an unforgettable trip.

Use periods of bright sun to scout from high vantages. That's when the shallows really light up and are easily distinguished from the darker deep-water zones. From a few hundred feet above a lake on a sunny day, you can easily see the location, shape, and extent of shallow flats, including small flats and rock humps that are a bit too deep to be seen readily from lake level. When you descend to the lake, you know exactly where to concentrate your spotting efforts. Even when you're in fishing position, scan and cast from the highest possible vantages. You'll spot many trout from 5 feet above the water that you won't see from a low angle, and from 20 feet above a clear mountain lake, you can spot trout cruising on the bottom in 10 or 15 feet of water well out from shore. On frigid high-altitude lakes, I often enjoy my best flats fishing on sunny afternoons when spotting conditions are ideal and the shallows warm sufficiently to activate the food chain.

Many high lakes are rimmed partially or entirely by shallow shelves that drop abruptly into deep water. Shelves offer cruising trout the best of both worlds—the abundant food of the shallows and quick access to the security of deep water. Watch for trout cruising parallel to shore over the outside edges of shelves, especially on lakes that have a shortage of flats. Where a shelf intersects a feeding flat, you'll often see heavy trout traffic. Shallow flats, large and small, are always worth checking for cruising fish. Flats adjacent to inlet and outlet streams are prime feeding and spawning areas and merit special attention.

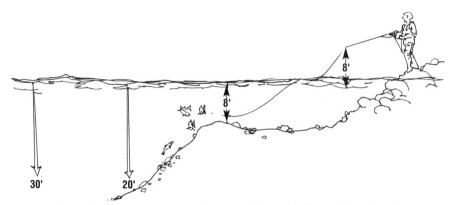

Many alpine lakes are rimmed partially or entirely by shallow shelves that drop abruptly into deep water. Shelves offer cruising trout the best of both worlds—the abundant food of the shallows and quick access to the security of deep water. From an elevated vantage point, you'll spot many cruising trout that you won't see from lake level.

I've had spectacular sight fishing for alpine trout by matching hatches and skating prospecting drys, but more often than not, big, healthy trout cruise fast and close to the bottom. For deep cruisers, I usually rig with a floating line, 12-foot leader with 4 feet of 4X tippet, and my Fast-Sinking Scud in size 12. I designed the scud to drop quickly to the level of deep-cruising fish without any additional weight. It casts like a bullet, even on a long tippet that enhances sink rate. I've taken more trophy-class trout from high lakes on the Fast-Sinking Scud than on all other patterns combined.

Spotting a cruiser and dropping the scud directly in its path is the name of the game. The deeper the fish and the faster it's moving, the farther you have to lead it. Big goldens typically cruise fast and deep, appearing as fleeting, blue-green apparitions. Big brook trout often cruise slower, with more serpentine routes close to the bottom. If a deep-cruising trout is within a foot or two of the bottom, it's often easier to see the dark shadow that the fish casts than it is to see the trout itself.

As the scud sinks into the path of a trout, I watch for the fish to veer or accelerate. This would mean the trout has seen the fly and I allow it to keep dropping, which trout find very enticing. If the fish stops in the vicinity of the scud, this usually means it has taken the fly, and I set the hook promptly. If a cruiser does not appear to see the fly or seems to be ignoring it, I strip the scud a bit as the fish is approaching and watch its reaction. If the fish shows interest, I keep stripping. If the trout doesn't strike or see the fly, a floating line allows for a long-line pickup, sometimes letting me get a second shot before it disappears. My stripping pattern and speed are dictated by the fish's response. I've seen trout rip a scud retrieved at a fast, steady clip, but other times a slow, erratic strip is the ticket.

When spotting conditions deteriorate on high lakes, I often prospect blindly over productive flats where I've previously seen cruising fish, using an attractor version of the Fast-Sinking Scud that I call the Mega Scud. I tie it in size 8 in various shades of pink and orange, with a silver flashback to make it highly visible to fish. I work it close to the bottom on an active strip to attract attention. On my second trip to Lightning Lake, the wind kicked up glacial flour that was very slow to settle, and the spotting conditions were lousy. In fact, I could not even see the small flat where I took the pair of big goldens on my earlier trip. Fortunately I knew the flat was there, because the Mega Scud produced more than a dozen good goldens from it. When I'm forced to prospect blindly on high lakes—when the water is clouded with suspended silt, wave action or low light makes it difficult to spot fish, or I'm forced to prospect deep—the Mega Scud often makes the difference between boom and bust. Brook trout, in particular, hammer an orange Mega Scud, so I often fish the pattern to visible brookies.

Sight fishing isn't just for alpine lakes. It can be equally effective on sprawling western reservoirs, the Great Lakes, and local lakes and spring ponds—wherever water clarity is good and trout cruise the flats and shorelines.

One of the great advantages of fishing to visible cruisers is that you can observe how they respond to your offerings. Keep experimenting. Once

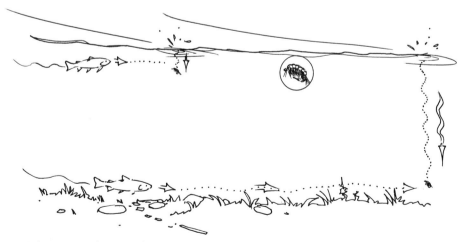

The Fast-Sinking Scud is designed to drop quickly into the path of a cruising trout. The deeper and faster a trout is cruising, the farther you have to lead it.

you find the right fly and presentation for a given lake, they can be good for a lot of nice trout.

WAKING THE SURFACE

It was a typical August day above timberline. Morning broke without a cloud in the sky, but massive thunderheads were building over the peaks by noon as hot air from the outlying basins lifted and cooled. I spent much of the afternoon hunkered down while thunder and lightning bombarded the immediate area and strong winds buffeted my tent. In the evening, the basins cooled and the thunderheads dissipated, and the lake I was camped on went glassy smooth. It felt good to get out of the tent and go fishing. I took one look at the dead-calm lake, reflecting the surrounding ridges and snowfields in eerie detail, and knotted on a Soft-Hackle Woolly Worm. I began waking the surface, which soon boiled as if a big smallmouth bass had sucked in a deerhair bug, but the fish I was into was much hotter than any smallmouth, with higher leaps, more speed, longer runs, deeper dives, much more endurance. For the next few hours, right into dark, I tore up what is possibly the best golden trout lake in the world by stripping the nymph just subsurface. Powerfully built goldens of 16 to 19 inches were the norm. The last fish of the day was a slab-sided buck that taped 23 inches and was a stunning deep crimson across his entire sides and belly. I'd toted a 60-pound pack more than 500 miles in my seven trips to the lake, and that golden was one of the biggest, and definitely the most beautiful, I'd caught there.

I've enjoyed a lot of fast action on alpine lakes by waking lively attractor nymphs across glassy surfaces on dead-calm evenings. It's a technique that also plays well on big lakes, spring ponds, beaver flowages, and the calm flats of streams and rivers—wherever you find smooth water and aggressive trout. I wake the surface frequently on the smooth flats of local spring creeks when trout are charged up. It's a great technique for prospecting rivers right at dark, when trout become more dependent on locating prey by sound. I've even seen it work on tailwater trout that supposedly won't hit anything but a tiny nymph on a perfect dead drift.

Waking the surface is very basic fishing. In fact, it's my favorite technique for shallow-water bluegills. All you need is a floating line, an unweighted tippet, and a soft, buggy nymph that pushes a visible wake as it's stripped just subsurface. On glassy water, trout see and hear that disturbance from a wide radius, and they home in on the visible wake. In good spotting conditions, I frequently see trout tear across many feet of water to smack the fly. In harsh glare or in flat evening light, when its tough to see through the surface, I often watch for the bulge created by a good trout closing rapidly on the nymph. When you see a big trout or an impressive bulge moving swiftly toward your fly, the natural tendency is to set the hook too early. You have to tame that tendency. Fortunately, when this technique is clicking, trout usually make a lot of hard charges, giving you ample opportunity to get it right.

BUOYANT BOTTOM FLIES

Even in July, the weather at 10,000 feet is a crapshoot. One evening atop the Beartooth Plateau, it was raw and windy with the lake rolling and gray clouds obscuring the surrounding peaks. I zipped my raincoat over my fleece jacket and went out to probe the cold, dark depths for fat brook trout. I picked a shore that put the wind at my back and launched the first double haul of the evening. When my sinking fly line reached bottom, I started to strip my fly—an orange Mega Scud with a buoyant closed-cell foam underbody. With each strip, the fly dived toward the line bellied on the lake bottom. With each pause, the buoyant fly ascended a few feet, lifting the tippet. It was a remarkably efficient and snag-free method of staying in close contact with the bottom over a long retrieve, even though I had only a vague idea of depth at any given point. Halfway through the retrieve the line felt heavy, and I set with a big sweep of the rod and a sharp downward haul of my line hand. My reward was a 17-inch brook trout with remarkable girth—one of many fine brookies that grabbed a buoyant bottom fly over the next few days.

Sinking fly lines and buoyant flies are tailor-made for probing lake bottoms for long distances with few hangups. That gives them a ton of applications for fishing all kinds of gamefish, especially in clean, weedless zones where you can slide the line right along the bottom. I enjoy canoeing the lakes of northern Wisconsin, northern Minnesota, and southern Ontario, and using a sinking line and buoyant baitfish imitation is by far my most productive technique for big smallmouth bass and walleyes. It's a great prospecting technique for large lakes, and I use it while casting, paddle trolling, and drifting with the wind.

Nymphs, streamers, and baitfish imitations can all be tied with buoyant closed-cell foam foundations. The bulkier the fly, the more closed-cell foam it will accommodate in the foundation and the quicker it will lift off bottom. A fast lift allows you to strip at a rapid tempo, working the fly erratically along the bottom, covering a lot of territory, and grabbing the

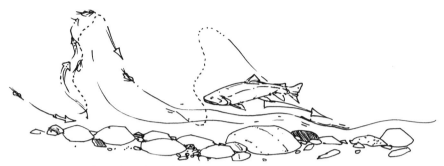

Buoyant nymphs and sinking fly lines are great for probing the critical bottom zone with few hang-ups. Belly the line on the lake bottom below the nymph. The nymph dives with each strip, following the path of the line, and rises off the bottom with each pause.

attention of fish from a distance—all great prospecting attributes. I usually add flash to my buoyant bottom flies to make them more visible in the dimly lit depths.

For working buoyant flies near the bottom, I primarily use full-sink lines with fast sink rates to put the line down pretty quickly in 10 to 30 feet of water. Ideally, you want the sinking line to belly on the bottom below the fly. The fly moves toward the bottom with each strip, following the path of the line, and rises off bottom rubble with each pause, positioning it for the next strip. Leader length, stripping speed and length, and fly's buoyancy all enter into how far the fly lifts off the bottom during a pause in the retrieve. Fish love to grab the fly on the rise; when they do that, the line will typically feel somewhat heavy as you begin the next strip. When you feel that heaviness, make a big sweeping hook set as you haul down with your rod hand—you need to move a lot of line to drive the hook home.

SUSPENDER NYMPHING

When stillwater trout are feeding selectively on small organisms, including midge pupae and plankton, you may need to drop way down in fly size to get strikes with any consistency. Trout may work emerging midge pupae from just subsurface to several feet down. If they are working right at the surface, I usually present without an indicator to avoid spooking the fish. I present the nymph with no shot or a single tiny one and strip slowly, detecting strikes by feel.

If trout are midging several feet below the surface, I usually run one or two tiny shot to suspend a micronymph vertically beneath a Palsa strike indicator—precisely the same rig I use to micronymph tailwaters and spring creeks—then adjust the indicator's depth until I find the most productive level. Once the micronymph is suspended, I usually creep it along, moving it just enough to attract a little attention.

Trout that feed primarily on plankton often follow it into the depths as bright sun drives it downward in the water column. Suspending a tiny micronymph vertically beneath a buoyant indicator on a very long leader can be effective on plankton feeders. Once the fly is suspended in the depths, I usually pulse it slowly to cover a bit of water. I rarely attempt to prospect large areas with this rig—I fish it primarily where I've located fish that aren't responding well to larger flies.

For suspending micronymphs on long leaders, a float tube or other craft is a major advantage, as it largely eliminates the need to cast. You can just pay out line as you drift or paddle. On high lakes, I do find opportunities to suspend very deep where deep water is close to shore.

To land a trout with an indicator positioned 20 or 30 feet up the leader, you need one that cranks through the rod guides or releases and slides down the leader when it hits the tip guide. When micronymphs will be suspended deeply, I often use an indicator that is a short section of poly yarn treated with floatant. I thread the yarn right through the middle loop of a blood knot before I cinch the knot tight. When I'm landing fish, the yarn cranks through the guides easily.

CHAPTER 9

Designing Active Nymphs

Tying your own flies allows you to control every variable: materials, silhouette, weight, color, size, hook style. This gives you the ability to design flies that are tailored to the waters you fish and your style of fishing—no small advantage.

Designing potent flies is not necessarily about creating entirely new patterns. Many of my bread-and-butter designs are variations on existing patterns—I've simply substituted superior materials or modified the tying technique to produce flies that fish to their full potential.

At the design stage, I always look critically at the materials and silhouette, which largely determine how a pattern looks and acts in the water. Color, size, and weight are secondary elements that are easily controlled. Once I've worked out a design that performs, I then run it up and down the scale in size, color, and weight for a range of applications.

Most of the flies I fish regularly—nymphs, drys, streamers, baitfish imitations, bass bugs—are my designs or significant variations on established patterns. I also tie these flies commercially and market them directly to anglers around the country. To request a mail-order fly catalog, write to Rich Osthoff, N6868 Sandstone Drive, Mauston, WI 53948.

ATTRACTOR NYMPHS

As I write this in early April, spring has sprung in southwestern Wisconsin. The three significant snows that fell in late March have swiftly dwindled to a few dirty patches in the shaded hollows. Last Sunday afternoon, after a morning of writing, I tossed the fishing gear in the car and drove to a local spring creek with my son in tow. Dale is eleven and the UPS truck recently delivered his first pair of waders—boys' size 4. I think Dale was more fired up to walk in the water than to fish. For the first hour, he threw a small, barbless spinner—the type with a revolving brass blade, not the type with gossamer wings. The stream was on the small side and not easy for a kid to spin, and Dale's luck was not as good as it's been on some larger streams. On our second swing away from the car, we left the spinning rod behind, and I got things going pretty well on an attractor nymph. As the water temperature climbed, I started getting an aggressive strike, or two or three, in nearly every good-looking little run. Dale played and helped release the first wild browns of the season, including some nicely colored fish in the 14-inch class.

Two days later, with Dale in school, I cut short another day of writing (what the heck, it was my birthday) and spent the afternoon checking out some different areas on the same stream. It was another fine spring day that warmed to a soft 70 degrees. Turkeys gobbled, a lone grouse drummed, the frogs in the side sloughs were almost deafening, and I flushed several mating pairs of wood ducks. Again, the trout were very aggressive subsurface. And again, I fished only a single fly pattern that afternoon—a lively attractor nymph.

That will soon change. On the first blustery outing, I expect to see blue-winged olives emerging, possibly mixed with midges. Sunny afternoons in late April will have the Grannom caddis popping. Some of our local streams have good cranefly hatches in early May, and a straggly, thinned-out Elk Hair Caddis is taken confidently by the rising fish. In May and June, the main mayfly hatches will fire up. By late June, the trout will be sipping beetles. By August, the hoppers will be taking wing. I'm shooting for a late-summer trip to the Rockies with Dale. Last summer on a family trip out west, Dale was in his glory scrambling around the exotic terrain of the Badlands, the Bighorns, Yellowstone, and a spectacular valley high in the Tetons that struck him as straight out of *Lord of the Rings.* I think Dale is ready for a few days above timberline in the Wind River Range, and we'll day-hike and fish some other places on that trip.

It should be an interesting season with a variety of angling, but I doubt I'll spend more than a third of my fishing time matching hatches or prospecting with dry flies. The bulk of the time I'll be working subsurface, mostly prospecting with an attractor nymph in a single pattern. Nearly all of the 2-pound and better trout that I land or lose on local spring creeks will grab that one attractor pattern. And that same nymph will see regular duty on the western trip. That is all as predictable as the robins returning, the apple orchards blossoming, and the whitetail does dropping their fawns.

I truly enjoy matching hatches and working to highly selective fish, and I carry a range of imitative fly patterns, many of which I've put considerable time and effort into developing. But the most valuable fly in my trout boxes is not anatomically correct, shadow-box beautiful, or wispy and ephemeral. It looks more like something the cat coughed up after a dank summer night in the woods. Even its name assaults the fly fisher's ear with that most repugnant of all nouns: *worm*. I call it the Soft-Hackle Woolly Worm.

Nearly thirty years ago, when I determined that bait and hardware were not in my fishing future and quit them cold turkey, I had my first transcendent fly-fishing experience on a local spring creek with a standard Woolly Worm. It was tied as the vast majority of flies sold in the United States are now tied—with cheap foreign labor by somebody who will never fly-fish. The setting was Castle Rock Creek on a soft, rainy Easter Sunday, and the trout went berserk. I could see them splashing all around me in the off-color water; soon I too learned to call it "rising." I was unschooled in the art of the drag-free dead drift and in the selective ways of wild brown trout—and so, apparently, were the fish, because I just slapped the line on the water and dragged the Woolly Worm around, and the trout slammed it. I took a dozen solid browns from one run.

At the time, I was buying my flies for cost plus 10 percent from the gun and sport shop where I worked, and on Monday morning right after punching the time clock and before unlocking the front door, I snapped up all the Brown & Brown Woolly Worms left in the bin—full-paying customers could just wait a few weeks for the next shipment.

I fished for a few years before beginning to tie, and I tied sporadically and at the hack level for a few years before getting more serious. Then I tied mostly standard stuff for a few years before starting to tweak patterns for my own fishing. Meanwhile, I was taking leave or quitting my job each June and backpacking and hitchhiking the Rockies for a few hundred bucks a summer, fishing a lot of great backcountry water and getting my feet wet in famed rivers like the Green, the Madison, and the Yellowstone. A standard Woolly Worm remained one of my standard prospecting nymphs, especially on lakes where actively stripping it produced many trout, including my first big goldens. But as I became a more astute tier, I recognized that the materials used in the standard pattern were wanting. The wool tail, chenille body, and rooster saddle hackle were stiff and lifeless, and the hackle virtually disappeared in low light or off-color water.

The catalyst to rebuild the Woolly Worm was my first Metz hen neck, which I picked up in the early 1980s at George Anderson's fly shop in Livingston, Montana. Like other hen necks, it had soft and webby hackle, but unlike other hen necks, its individual feathers were long—long enough to palmer several times around a chunky prospecting nymph.

With the right hackle in hand, I knew I could build a better Woolly, and I overhauled the rest of the fly while I was at it. For the tail, I scrapped the standard wool and settled on a tuft of soft underfur and guard hairs clipped from a rabbit hide. For the body, instead of chenille, I used a dubbing blend of two-thirds rabbit and one-third chopped Antron for added sparkle. Dubbing greatly improved the fuzziness and sheen of the nymph and allowed me to build a body with a nice forward taper. It also increased the time required to tie the fly, especially in larger sizes. I eventually found a way to speed up the process by building a yarn foundation and then dubbing over it. UNI-Thread now markets UNI-Yarn, which works perfectly for quickly wrapping a tight, smooth foundation.

Though the feathers from the Metz hen cape were quite long, in order to palmer an entire size 12 body with a single feather, I had to pluck one from high on the cape, which gave me much longer hackle barbules than I wanted. I quickly discovered that I could keep the hackle reasonably short and mirror the tapered profile of the dubbed body by palmering two hackle feathers: a shorter one with shorter barbules over the rear half of the body, and a longer one with longer barbules over the front half.

Before removing the nymph from the vise, I raked it with a stiff nylon brush to sweep and distribute the hackle, rough up the dubbed fur body, and marry the hackle and fur into a blurred and tantalizing whole. I held my handiwork up to the tying light and moaned softly. It was the start of a twenty-year relationship that is still going strong. I had created a nymph that begged to be moved, and it wound up schooling me in the neglected art of moving the nymph.

The Soft-Hackle Woolly Worm has become my top prospecting nymph by a runaway margin because it has movement to burn. Short of ripping it past trout with accelerating drag, there is really no wrong way to fish it, and there is no way to still it. It moves and pulsates beautifully on a dead drift or very slow strip. It moves seductively under controlled drag. I get many strikes while staccato stripping slowly through deep runs and pools with the tip of a floating fly line submerged and dragging a bit. It flares and appears to breathe as it is stripped or swung. And exceptional movement is just one of the fly's super prospecting attributes.

This pattern presents a bold silhouette when viewed from any angle— head-on, broadside, or going away. When you're actively moving the nymph and presenting at all angles, that's a vital attribute. In true prospecting, when you're trying to locate trout and grab their attention, you don't want a nymph whose visibility is greatly diminished if it's not viewed broadside.

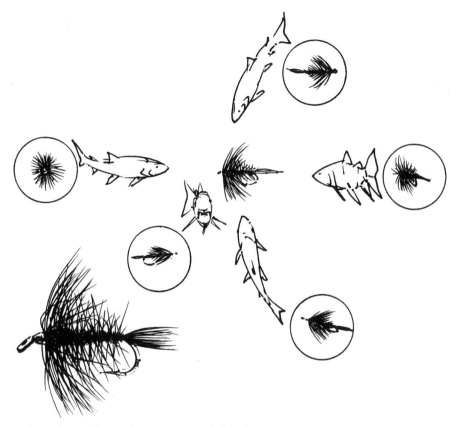

The Soft-Hackle Woolly Worm cuts a bold silhouette when viewed from any angle—a vital attribute in a true prospecting nymph.

The hen hackle is webby enough to maintain a bold silhouette in all water and lighting conditions, yet light penetrates to the body and diffuses through the fuzzed-out dubbing to create a halo of translucency that strongly suggests life. Brushing—really raking the dubbing—to create soft, fuzzy margins is an integral element of many of my nymph designs. I tease with a brush meant for cleaning gun parts, not a bore brush. You can buy the brush in gun shops or order it out of gunsmithing catalogs under several brand names. It looks like a toothbrush on one end, and the other end tapers down to support a single row of short, stiff nylon bristles that are ideal for raking vigorously right over hackle stems, wing cases, and ribbing materials without doing damage. The brush operates in a blur, quickly teasing the entire body, if that's your objective. It is also ideal for directional teasing and for flattening nymph profiles. When trying my Fuzzy Hare's

Ear nymph, for example, I overdub the thorax, then brush hard from under the thorax up toward the edges of the wing case to project guard hairs and soft underfur from the sides to simulate legs. I also brush up toward the sides of the abdomen to simulate gill filaments. When a trout is really eye-balling a nymph in slow current, that subtle movement of brushed-out materials can seal the deal. Brushing upward from underneath also flattens the pattern into a blocky clinger-crawler mayfly nymph profile.

The Soft-Hackle Woolly Worm is potent in a wide range of sizes. I tie it in 2 to 16. Size 12 sees the most action on trout—it's small enough to be presented precisely on light trout rods, yet substantial enough to consistently move top-end trout.

The fly can be tied in a range of natural or attractor colors. I primarily use grizzly hackle for its sheer fish appeal, but for dirty water, I usually go with black. For bodies and tails, I stick mostly to black and other dark natural shades like brown and olive. A dark fly maintains a bold silhouette in low light or deep or dirty water—conditions that beg for an effective prospecting nymph. With attractor colors, the sky's the limit, but the pattern fishes so well in natural shades, and suggests life in general so well, that I haven't experimented widely with loud colors that do not occur frequently in prey. An all-black Woolly with an orange tail is the one loud color I routinely carry. My brother Eric caught a couple of his largest spring creek browns on the orange tail, and I've noticed that browns and brookies really like it in September as spawning on our local creeks is fast approaching or just getting started. It's also a great color on the high lakes; goldens, cutthroats, and rainbows are all springtime spawners that commonly spawn into July up around timberline, and they seem to respond well to the orange tail into August, when I do most of my high-lake fishing. Here's the formula for tying the design in any color.

SOFT-HACKLE WOOLLY WORM

Hook:	Tiemco 5262 or 5263 (2XL or 3XL nymph hook).
Thread:	6/0.
Weight:	Wire wrapped around the hook shank at the thorax as desired.
Tail:	Tuft of fur and guard hairs clipped from a rabbit hide or a zonker strip. My tails are at least half the body length. A finished tail can be shortened or thinned at any time by simply plucking it down with your fingers.

Underbody: UNI-Yarn. Color is irrelevant; the foundation shouldn't be visible on the finished fly. The purpose of the yarn foundation is to reduce dubbing time on large nymphs. For sizes 14 and 16, I omit the underbody.

Body: Blend rabbit underfur and guard hairs with about one-third clear Antron fibers. Chop synthetic fibers very short, or they will lock around the tying thread and will not tease out readily.

Hackle: Two generic hen hackles. I primarily use Metz and Whiting hen necks, but any generic hen neck with feathers long enough to palmer three or four turns is suitable.

1. Wrap weighting wire and secure it with thread.
2. Tie in tail. Leave the thread bobbin at tail position. That clears operating room for step 3.
3. Wrap the yarn underbody, running the yarn on a separate bobbin. To attach the yarn, simply trap it under itself, just like starting thread on a hook. I attach right over the weighting wire and wrap a fatter foundation over the thorax before wrapping a thinner foundation back to the tail. When you reach the tail position, pick up the thread bobbin and make a pass forward and back over the yarn foundation to reinforce it with crisscrossing wraps. Snip the yarn; you're done with that bobbin.
4. Tie in the smaller hackle by the tip at the bend; barbule length should equal or slightly exceed the hook gap. Dub the rear half of the body; taking the first turn of dubbing behind the hackle tie-in point. Leave the thread bobbin at midshank. Palmer the first hackle forward over the rear half of the body. As you wind forward, barbule length will increase from short to long to complement the forward taper of the body. To avoid breaking stem tips, always wrap the first turn of hackle with moderate tension. On subsequent turns, the hackle stem should be firmly seated into the dubbing. Tie off the hackle and snip the stem butt.
5. Tie in the larger hackle by the tip at the dubbing break; barbule length should be one and a half to two times the hook gap. Dub the front half of the body, and palmer the second hackle forward over it. Tie off the hackle stem at the head and trim the stem butt. Build a smooth thread head and whip-finish.

6. Leaving the nymph in the vise, brush from head to tail on all sides to sweep and distribute the hackle and marry it with teased-out dubbing fibers. The bigger the fly, the more dramatic the effects of vigorous brushing. Apply head cement.

I tie Soft-Hackle Woolly Buggers in the same sequence on the same nymph hooks. For Buggers, I stick with the traditional body-length marabou tail, using the tips of marabou blood quills. I tie six to eight strands of flash material (I like Holographic Flashabou) into the tail. I increase hackle length on the front half of the body to about twice the hook gap. To achieve lots of web and long enough hackle on a size 8 or larger fly, I usually hackle the front half with a feather from a hen saddle or body rather than a neck.

Since the Soft-Hackle Woolly Worm and Bugger are dubbed and hackled in two stages, it's easy to switch color schemes at the dubbing break. That quirk in the tying procedure gave birth to the Bi-Bugger. You can go wild with the Bi-Bugger concept to create colorful attractor flies for everything from pike to bass to steelhead. Red-white, green-yellow, and black-orange are just a few combinations. The Bi-Bugger that I fish extensively on trout is designed to mimic crayfish and sculpin color schemes. The tail is black marabou over olive marabou with gold flash. The rear half of the body is grizzly hackle palmered over olive dubbing, and the front half is black hackle palmered over black dubbing. The Bi-Bugger in that color scheme is flat nasty on adult brown trout. I tie it with lead eyes and hop it on lakes and streams, and smallmouth bass pounce on it. It's a killer carp fly; if you're ever in the vicinity of Flaming Gorge Reservoir with a few hours to kill, try sight-fishing the Bi-Bugger to the huge carp that cruise the clear shorelines. My steelhead experience is limited to Wisconsin streams running into Lake Michigan, but the black-olive-grizzly Bi-Bugger has easily been my best steelhead fly.

Woolly Buggers are generally classified as streamers, but when tied to their full potential with soft, webby hen hackle and teased-out, dubbing they move like a dream, even on a dead drift, and cut a strong silhouette when viewed head-on. Most streamer patterns are weak on both counts—they dead drift stiffly and have a weak profile when seen from any direction but broadside. That really hamstrings their effectiveness for upstream presentations in current, which pretty much kills them as small-stream prospecting flies. In my view, this is such a versatile and productive prospecting streamer precisely because it has so many great nymph and wet-fly characteristics. Dead drifting, lifting, swinging, stripping, dragging, viewable from any side, presentable at any angle in any current speed—the design has no weaknesses, only strengths. And tying this fly with soft hen hackle and teased-out dubbing rather than the standard materials takes all of those strengths to another level.

However these flies in general are classified, the Soft-Hackle Woolly Bugger is perfectly suited to active nymphing tactics. I fish the Soft-Hackle Bugger much as I fish the Soft-Hackle Worm, which I classify as a nymph with wet-fly hackle. The biggest difference in how I fish the two is *when* I fish them. If the water is clear and I know trout are readily seeing the fly, then I prospect with the Woolly Worm in size 12 to 16; it's a little more subtle, and it casts more precisely and sinks faster with less weight. Since I fish a lot of small spring creeks, where precise delivery and total control of the fly in the water is important, I fish this pattern more. If the water is dirty, I'm specifically targeting large trout, or I'm prospecting sizable water with a low trout density, then I usually go with the Woolly Bugger in size 8 or larger to put flash and longer hackle into play, boosting the visibility of my prospecting pattern. I do tie Mini-Buggers right down into nymph sizes 12 and 14 for precise presentations with light rods on small streams, and I regularly fish them when local spring creeks are roiled. The biggest difference I notice in how these two patterns fish is that I get more short hits on Buggers from small to average trout. I save my chewed-up Mini-Buggers for panfishing. Panfish crave the action of small Buggers and suction them in, tail and all, with no problem. Plus, I pick up quite a few largemouth bass on them while targeting panfish.

I don't prospect with any other attractor nymphs as much as I do with the Soft-Hackle Woolly Worm. Attractor nymphing is about attraction and simulating life in general, not precise imitation. You don't need to simulate umpteen different organisms. You just need a single design that grabs the attention of trout, looks unequivocally alive, and performs in a broad range of sizes.

One of the beauties of attractor nymphing extensively with a single pattern is that you really learn the subtleties of fishing that particular pattern. You develop a feel for how to cast it, how fast it sinks, how deep it is at any given moment, and how and when to move it. You've spent so many hours and days and seasons probing with that one pattern knotted to your tippet that from run to run, you begin to make very subtle adjustments almost intuitively—and in nymphing, the subtle adjustments are usually the key adjustments. When you have an attractor nymph that has great prospecting attributes *and* you fish it with a sixth sense, that's when your prospecting really takes off.

Given the wealth of materials and the many fine tiers that are out there, others might start with similar parameters and come up with an attractor nymph that is quite different from the Soft-Hackle Woolly Worm. Here are some of the characteristics to consider as you sit down at the vise to design a potent attractor nymph for general prospecting on your home waters and in your travels: You want a fly that is substantial enough to consistently move top-end trout yet small enough to present precisely; cuts a bold silhouette when viewed from any angle; looks absolutely alive on a dead drift and when it's activated; fishes well in fast water yet fools trout in slow water where they can really eyeball a substantial fly; remains potent in sizes 2 to 16 to adapt to a wide range of applications and water conditions; and grabs the attention of trout yet looks entirely natural.

IMITATIVE NYMPHS

I carry a full range of imitative nymphs and emergers—mayfly nymphs, caddis pupae, midge pupae—but rarely employ them for searching the water for scattered trout. I tend to use them on selective trout I've already located, during emergences, and for match-the-drift fishing on exceptionally fertile tailwaters and spring creeks where trout densities are sky high and even large fish are accustomed to grazing on steady streams of small organisms. On less fertile waters, I fish them in prime zones where I know trout will readily see even a small imitative nymph.

I often activate imitative nymphs, but subtly, such as when pulsing a mayfly nymph pattern to mimic the swimming or ascending motions of the natural. I don't dart and strip them as vigorously as I sometimes move attractor nymphs. There's no need to—I'm presenting right to fish and attempting to fool them, rather trying to grab their attention and move them.

In my view, attractor nymphs should be tied robustly with plenty of soft materials to create seductive movement that is visible at a distance. Small imitative nymphs are another matter. In proportion and silhouette, they should more closely resemble the slight organisms they mimic, and too much material of any kind tends to build bulk and make them less convincing. When you're presenting small imitative nymphs directly to discriminating trout, a bit of inherent movement from the materials to help create the illusion of life upon close inspection is all you need.

Brushing your dubbed nymphs teases out guard hairs, soft underfur, and synthetic fibers to simulate legs and gills that move a bit, enhancing the realism of the fly on close inspection. There are very few dubbed nymphs or emergers that I don't brush to some degree. For most of my patterns, I chop and mix my own dubbings, controlling the percentage of guard hairs, underfur, and synthetics, to achieve specific brushing results. I can chop synthetic fibers short so they tease out along with the natural fibers.

Brushing can be quite radical, as on the Fuzzy Hare's Ear. Squirrel body-hair blends are great for dubbing exceptionally spiky nymphs with grizzled highlights. Directional brushing can create different silhouettes. By over-dubbing a bit and then brushing vigorously in controlled directions, you can flatten nymph profiles and cause teased-out dubbing to project directly from the sides. Brushing can also be subtle. I tie my Floating Nymphs, which I always carry in a range of sizes to imitate emerging mayflies, with a pronounced foam wing case pulled forward over the dubbed thorax and tied off at the head, like a standard quill wing case. I dub the bodies mini-mally and then hit them lightly with the brush to fuzz them just a bit.

Soft hackle can be used minimally to create tails and legs that move a bit in the current without distorting the proportions or profiles of small imitative nymphs. Fuzzy herl materials, such as ostrich and peacock, look and move much like natural gills.

On micronymph patterns, I rarely strive for built-in movement from the materials; convincing silhouette and proportion are more important factors for diminutive flies. My best all-around micronymph, the Pheasant-Tail Midge, is wrapped with just two to four pheasant-tail fibers tied in by the tips near the hook bend. The abdomen is reinforced with fine copper wire, which is tied off and clipped at the front. The thorax is a couple more turns of the same pheasant-tail fibers. Natural ring-necked pheasant tail produces a thorax that is darker than the abdomen as you wind into the darker portion of the fiber butts. I tie most of my Pheasant-Tail Midges using natural ring-necked or black pheasant tail, the latter obtained from melanistic birds that are used on some shooting preserves.

Scuds and fairy shrimp are quick, agile swimmers. On lakes, I often strip imitations rapidly to imitate fleeing crustaceans and grab the attention of fish. The Fast-Sinking Scud was the breakthrough pattern that really increased my percentage of hookups when sight-casting to trophy trout on high lakes. I fished the high country for several summers before I had that fly, and I jokingly refer to those summers as B.S.—Before Scud. Friction between the water and raked-out dubbing causes the fly to flip onto its smooth back and sink quickly. I originally designed the pattern for a fast sink rate so it would drop quickly in front of trout cruising several feet below lake surfaces, but it has also become my standard scud imitation for spring creeks. Here's the tying formula.

FAST-SINKING SCUD

Hook:	Tiemco 3761 (1XL wet-fly hook).
Thread:	6/0.
Weight:	About ten wraps of wire the same diameter as hook shank.
Shellback:	Clear elastic or Scud Back. I use Stretchrite Clear Elastic, which is sold in fabric departments in 5-yard strips that are ⅜-inch wide. For size 14 and larger shellbacks, split the material up the middle with sharp scissors to produce ³⁄₁₆-inch strips. For size 16 and smaller, split the material again. A dozen or more shellbacks can be tied from a 6-inch-long strip. The final width of the shellback is controlled by stretching the elastic as it's pulled over the body and tied off at the head. The body color shows through the clear elastic. Scud Back is a stretch elastic sold in various tints and widths. Elastic is much more durable than poly bag material and much faster to tie with, as shellbacks don't have to be cut out individually.
Tail:	About half a dozen pheasant-breast fibers. For olive-gray scuds, I use hen pheasant breast; for the orange scud, I use cock pheasant breast.
Underbody:	UNI-Yarn. Color is irrelevant; the foundation shouldn't be visible on the finished fly. The purpose of the yarn foundation is to reduce dubbing time. For sizes 14 and 16, I omit the underbody.
Body:	Blend rabbit underfur and guard hairs with about one-third clear Antron fibers. Chop synthetic fibers very short, or they will lock around the tying thread and will not tease out readily.
Ribbing:	Retired 4X or 5X tippet material, which bites and holds well on the elastic.

1. Wrap weighting wire over rear two-thirds of hook shank, and lock it down securely with thread wraps. The pattern is ribbed under a lot of tension, and if the weighting wire and yarn foundation are not tightly secured, the entire fly will rotate on the hook shank during ribbing.
2. Tie in tail at bend.

3. Tie in strip of clear elastic on top of tail securely so that it doesn't slip loose as it is stretched later. Leave the thread bobbin at the tail position to clear room for step 4.

4. Wrap the yarn underbody with a reverse taper, making it fatter toward the tail. Run the yarn on a separate bobbin. To attach the yarn, simply trap it under itself, just like starting thread on a hook. I attach right over the weighting wire and wrap a fatter foundation over the thorax before wrapping a thinner foundation back to the tail. After wrapping the foundation, pick up the thread bobbin and make a pass forward and back over the yarn foundation to reinforce it with crisscrossing wraps. Snip the yarn; you're done with that bobbin.

5. Tie in the ribbing material, leaving room to wrap some dubbing behind the first turn of ribbing or it will slip off the rear of the shellback during tying or fishing. Lash the ribbing material tightly to the yarn foundation so that it does not pull loose as the scud is ribbed under heavy tension.

6. Dub over the underbody. I dub a chunky body that is flattened during brushing.

7. Pull the shellback forward, tie off securely, and snip excess.

8. Wind ribbing forward under heavy tension so it bites into dubbing and shellback. Tie off ribbing at head and snip excess. Over time, I've seen elastic that I believe was damaged by contact with head cement, so I no longer cement the heads.

9. Rake vigorously with a stiff nylon brush from under belly up toward edges of shellback to flatten body and cause dubbing fibers to project from sides of fly.

AFTERWORD

In nymphing, as in most fly fishing, control of the fly is critical. Where the nymph hits the water, how it hits the water, and what you do (or don't do) to it after it hits the water largely govern your success.

Where the nymph hits the water is strictly a function of your casting skill. As you hone your abilities to sling weighted rigs with controlled loops at high line speeds, both accuracy and distance will follow.

How the nymph enters the water also depends on your casting skill. Nothing is accomplished by delivering a nymph right on target if the altitude of the line does not allow the nymph to drop to a productive depth. As you learn to control how the fly line, leader, and nymph hit the water, precise presentation, including fast vertical drops of the nymph to productive levels, will follow.

What you do or don't do once the nymph is in the water dictates how trout respond to it. Moving the nymph grabs the attention of predatory trout and often generates aggressive strikes, even from inactive fish. And active nymphing puts you in direct control of the speed, path, and behavior of the nymph.

Control. In dozens of ways, from major to subtle, nymphing actively increases your control of the fly in the air and in the water, allowing you to nymph virtually any water type from any angle of presentation with real efficiency. Moving the nymph, and moving it skillfully in very specific zones, is fly fishing at its best—visual, absorbing, technique-intensive, and extraordinarily productive.

Good fishing,
Rich Osthoff

INDEX

ABOUT THE AUTHOR

Rich Osthoff grew up fishing for trout on the spring creeks of south-western Wisconsin. He has fished extensively throughout the Rockies and has made well over a hundred backpacking trips to explore backcountry waters. Rich guides trout anglers in western Wisconsin. He ties his fly designs commercially and markets them directly to anglers, and he speaks frequently to fly-fishing clubs and gatherings.

Rich has written two other books, *Fly-Fishing the Rocky Mountain Backcountry* and *No Hatch to Match: Aggressive Strategies for Fly-Fishing between Hatches,* both published by Stackpole Books. His articles have appeared in *Flyfishing & Tying Journal, American Angler, Fly Tyer, Outdoor Life,* and other magazines.

Rich lives in Mauston, Wisconsin, with his wife, Dawn; son, Dale; and daughter, Dana.